D0690724

WRITING IN THE CONTENT AREAS

SECOND EDITION

Amy Benjamin
Hendrick Hudson High School

EYE ON EDUCATION
6 DEPOT WAY WEST, SUITE 106
LARCHMONT, NY 10538
(914) 833-0551
(914) 833-0761 fax
www.eyeoneducation.com

Copyright © 2005 Eye On Education, Inc.

All Rights Reserved.

For information about permission to reproduce selections from this book, write: Eye On Education, Permissions Dept., 6 Depot Way West, Suite 106, Larchmont, N.Y. 10538.

Library of Congress Cataloging-in-Publication Data

Benjamin, Amy, 1951-
  Writing in the content areas / Amy Benjamin.— 2nd ed.
    p. cm.
  Includes bibliographical references.
  ISBN 1-59667-002-9
    1. English language—Composition and exercises—Study and teaching
  (Secondary) 2. Language arts—Correlation with content subjects. I. Title.
  LB1631.B385 2005
  808'.042'0712—dc22

                                                                    2005000930

Editorial and production services provided by
UB Communications, 10 Lodge Lane, Parsippany, NJ 07054
(973-331-9391)

Also available from Eye On Education

Differentiated Instruction:
A Guide for Middle and High School Teachers
Amy Benjamin

Differentiated Instruction:
A Guide for Elementary School Teachers
Amy Benjamin

Differentiated Instruction Using Technology:
A Guide for Middle and High School Teachers
Amy Benjamin

English Teacher's Guide to
Performance Tasks and Rubrics:
Middle School
Amy Benjamin

English Teacher's Guide to
Performance Tasks and Rubrics:
High School
Amy Benjamin

Handbook on Differentiated Instruction
For Middle and High Schools
Sheryn Spencer Northey

Socratic Seminars and Literature Circles
For Middle and High School English
Victor and Marc Moeller

What Great Teachers Do Differently
14 Things That Matter Most
Todd Whitaker

What Every Teacher Needs to Know about Assessment
Leslie Walker Wilson

Social Studies: Standards, Meaning & Understanding
Barbara Stern

Reading, Writing, and Gender:
Instructional Strategies and Activities That Work for Girls and Boys
Gail Goldberg and Barbara Roswell

FOREWORD

A workshop in early spring, mud season, in Montrose, New York, a wooded community near the Hudson River, was where I first met Amy Benjamin several years ago. Teachers, K-12, were struggling with realizing the state standards in writing with the realities of their own classrooms. I had worked with most of the group before, enjoyed their earnest desire to help students, and appreciated the humor they used to assist in communication between buildings. It was the first time I had met Amy. She spoke eloquently and passionately about a collaborative project she and a colleague had developed on the Holocaust. What struck me, however, was not only the clarity and freshness of her descriptions, but that in every sentence the role of students was primary. The most important outcome of work in writing should be manifest in the student's work. Amy's concern was that each teacher help his or her students become effective editors and revisers on the page.

In a range of subsequent settings I observed her remarkable ability to share highly specific strategies and teaching techniques. After one district meeting, a colleague of hers approached me and asked, "Did you know that Amy runs an inservice course on writing across the curriculum? She is amazing. I have seen a direct effect on my kid's work." In a sense, the book you have in your hands is a collegial coaching session, an inservice opportunity, on a problem that faces most teachers. As one second-year teacher put it, " Given all that I have to do in the classroom, how can I adjust my plans to produce stronger writers? Can these approaches be integrated into my daily plans?" Amy Benjamin gives us organized, focused, practical, and inventive practices to face this dilemma, whether you are a new or experienced teacher.

Writing in the Content Areas helps teachers in each discipline with applications targeted to the unique characteristics of specific departments. The book also provides a direct and useful tool for communication between departments, which is equally important in improving the quality of student writing. Amy Benjamin's book has made a substantive and inventive contribution to classroom teachers and to the writers in their classrooms.

Heidi Hayes Jacobs

TABLE OF CONTENTS

INTRODUCTION TO THE SECOND EDITION

When I wrote *Writing in the Content Areas* in 1998, people didn't go around suggesting to each other that they google things. Very few teachers directed students to WebQuests, although the form had been developed by Bernie Dodge and Tom March at San Diego State University by that time. I didn't maintain my own classroom Website, nor did I accept assignments through e-mail. I didn't use the language that I've come to call "e-speak" to transition students from informal to formal English.

Today I can't imagine functioning without my classroom Website, not accepting student writing through e-mail, and not responding to it with on-screen comments, including WebQuests, Hotlists, and Virtual Explorations as choices for students, and consulting the Internet for everything imaginable (including searches to check for plagiarism).

When I was writing this book, English teachers in New York State were scrambling to prepare students for what was to be known as the "All Regents High School," wherein every students would have to pass a marathon test requiring four essays in two different writing modes. Teachers in other subject areas were figuring out how to infuse writing instruction so that students could give constructed responses in complete sentences, in addition to traditional multiple choice and word-or-phrase answers.

Almost all states have required students to meet subject area standards that call for higher order thinking, the kind of thinking that is attended to, supported, and advanced by writing. The permeable membrane that I spoke about in the 1999 book is now the erasable membrane, as writing has become, in the words of the National Commission on Writing in America's Schools and Colleges, "everybody's business."

Although I've always believed strongly in the importance of teaching grammar as a way of facilitating communication about language between teachers and students, the need for teaching grammar is now in full ascendancy. The SAT is still a major factor in the college admissions process (in some places more than others, granted). And the SAT now, like the SAT II and the ACT, includes both an on-demand writing sample and a section requiring that students know how to edit sentences in standard written English.

We can reach our students in powerful ways by opening creative and sensory channels of the brain. Creative writing, along with creative dramatics, allows for durable learning, as students make interdisciplinary connections. Besides, stories, embedded as they are in time and place, carry information about science, social studies, and mathematics. We learn some of our most important lessons through stories, so why not invite our students to process information in story form?

The second edition of *Writing in the Content Areas* enriches the first edition by infusing the role of technology, especially word processing, presentation programming, the Internet, and e-communications, into instruction. This edition also offers teachers who have the layman's grasp of grammar instruction in how to get students to write meaningful, clear sentences by using templates. Like the first edition, the second edition is founded on the belief that time spent teaching writing is time well spent indeed, as writing itself reinforces and advances learning.

I've realized that English teachers as well as teachers of other content areas are reading this book. The Standards require us English teachers to make major forays into content area writing. No longer do we teach only the traditional genres associated with English Language Arts. We are teaching informational writing as well, in which the writer integrates numerical information with the content of sentences and paragraphs. Our job as English teachers is to teach students how to shift language registers to match message to audience, purpose, and context.

This second edition of *Writing in the Content Areas* brings in technology, differentiated instruction, brain-based learning, and more interdisciplinary experiences to help students become stronger thinkers and communicators through writing to as many audiences as possible.

PART I

STEPS AND STRATEGIES

1

GUIDING PRINCIPLES FOR TEACHERS

Let's begin by saying that if you are not an English teacher, I don't expect you to become one. And if you are an English teacher, I don't expect you to become something else. Because content area teachers have needs that differ from those of English teachers as far as student writing is concerned, I've divided the guiding principles into three parts: *For All Teachers; For Content Area Teachers; For English Teachers.* Let's remember that the term *content area teachers* is a convenient designation for those who teach subjects other than English. English, of course, has its own content: literary analysis and the study of language. In addition to this content, English teachers are expected to teach the skill of using the English language—in writing, reading, speaking, and listening—to achieve desired effects. Thus, if you are an English teacher, both sets of guiding principles would apply to what you do. If you teach a subject other than English, the set of guiding principles for content area teachers is probably all you need. In any case, the bedrock principle of this book is this: *Writing equips the mind to think.*

GUIDING PRINCIPLES FOR ALL TEACHERS

THE LEARNING CYCLE

I think of the learning cycle as having five components:

♦ **Introduction to new information**
  As the teacher, you lay the groundwork for new learning by activating prior knowledge as you link the familiar to the new. You establish expectations, perhaps by giving an outlined overview, essential questions, links to the students' own world, an anecdote, or anticipatory set (anecdotal metaphor that sparks interest, makes a connection, and establishes expectations). An informal writing experience, such as notes or a list, can activate prior knowledge. This introductory activity can form a baseline that will be compared to fuller learning about the subject later on.

3

♦ Presentation of new information

Because new information is best learned if we present it in more than one form, we might couple a lecture with a reading assignment. Experienced teachers keep the need for multisensory engagement in mind as they present new information. They include plenty of visuals, manipulatives, opportunities to have students speak the familiar and new language of the subject. Teachers make students particularly aware of new terminology and how to use it, modeling the new words in many contexts. It is at this point that students can build a word bank for the new information.

♦ Processing

If the information is appropriately challenging, students will need more than just input from an outside source (you and the text) to understand it. They need to process to make the information their own. The processing is usually done through language: questions and answers, problem-solving in a lab setting, labeling a map or diagram, constructing a model and explaining it. Writing is an extremely effective way to process, to come to own, new information. But the writing at this point in the learning cycle does not have to be formal, and I must emphasize this point. It's at the processing stage that students should be offered informal writing experiences: notes, loosely-structured outlines, annotations, lists. Writing at this phase of the learning cycle is called "writing to learn" or "writing your way into knowing." Writing leaves "brain prints," so to speak.

♦ Assessment

It's at the assessment phase that we traditionally think of writing. Here, we want students to answer questions in complete sentences, well-developed paragraphs, in-class essays, traditional research reports. And it is "assessment writing" that is most troublesome to us. What if I suspect that the student plagiarized or received undue assistance from a parent? What if the product is carelessly presented? What do I do about egregious offenses in spelling, capitalization, and grammar? If I don't teach English, how much weight should I give to a writing assessment? If I do teach English, is it appropriate to assign a topic that involves art history, stem cell research, or local politics? Teachers usually pick up a book like this because of their concerns about the kind of writing that is used for assessment. Writing at this phase of the learning cycle is called "writing to show what you know."

♦ Remediation or advancement

This phase of the learning cycle often doesn't happen. Unfortunately, we often skip right over the part where, after the assessment, the students get to strengthen demonstrated weaknesses or advance to the next level, having shown themselves capable of doing so. To reach this stage, teachers need to think of the assessment as diagnostic. Assessment that gives diagnostic information is called "formative assessment." Practitioners of differentiated instruction do bring students to this phase of the learning cycle.

WRITING IS CONNECTED TO READING, SPEAKING, AND LISTENING

Writing is the most intellectually demanding of the four modes of communication through language. Writing is the last of the four to be mastered. First we learn to understand spoken language; then, we learn to produce it through speech. Long after that, and usually only with a great deal of time and effort, do we learn to decode symbols and develop enough fluency to make meaning from them. But writing, encoding, has an even more sophisticated component than reading: writers have to figure out that writing conventions are stricter than those for speech. Fledgling writers often proclaim, "I write the way I speak." What they should be doing, however, is writing the way they *read*.

Obviously, writing is only going to be as good as it is substantial. Writers need a message. Before we expect students to be able to write anything about our subject, we have to see to it that they've *read* in the subject area. Conceive of writing as one of the four language components and understand the interdependency of the reading, writing, listening, and speaking.

The process of speaking is, for many learners, a process of speaking oneself into knowing. The learner may have to put the words in his or her own mouth to internalize the concepts. Hence, a classroom consisting predominantly of teacher talk will result in an imbalance in the four language components. Think of it as driving a car in only first gear.

STUDENTS RESPECT THE RIGOR OF CLASSES THAT DEMAND WRITING

Students know that writing is serious business. They may complain about having to write critiques in art class, self-reflections in music performance class, goals in physical education class, logs or journals in health class, process explanations in math class. But these complaints, complaints against unwelcome rigor, evidence the value of including writing: writing is serious business. "Writing is . . . a complex intellectual activity that requires students to stretch their minds, sharpen their analytical capabilities, and make valid and accurate distinctions." (*The Neglected R*. The College Board, 2002, p. 13).

EXPLICITLY TEACH THE FORM AND TONE THAT YOU EXPECT FOR A WRITING TASK

An effective way to do this is to present a model and go through the features of it that you want your students to emulate. Anyone who has ever walked unescorted through an unfamiliar art museum knows how that experience differs from the same walk with a knowledgeable, enthusiastic docent. Be that docent for your students: point out details and techniques that the uninformed eye would not notice.

GUIDING PRINCIPLES FOR INCLUDING WRITING IN THE CONTENT AREAS

YOU ARE NOT TEACHING WRITING: YOU ARE TEACHING YOUR SUBJECT

Corollary: Time spent including writing in your instruction is not time that you must "subtract" from subject area teaching.

When your students are writing something in or for your class, they are processing what they are supposed to learn in your subject. Writing is not just a demonstration of what has been learned (assessment); writing is a means to learn (process).

BE FLEXIBLE IN YOUR DEFINITION OF WRITING

Formal writing is *not* the only useful form of writing. As subject area specialists, we speak a certain language. It is our job to initiate the novice into the professional conversation. In other words, we want very much for students to use the proper terminology, terminology that we and the textbook explain and model. However, the only way for students to bring "our language" into their vernacular is to give them writing experiences that allow them to transition from the latter to the former. Listen to students as they work out a problem, such as a series of question-answers from the textbook. You will hear them mix technical terms with vernacular. We wouldn't expect them to speak as if they were professors delivering a prepared lecture. Nor would we expect them to answer the questions without using any of the proper terminology. Content area writing, at the processing stage, can operate the same way that speech does *if* we re-imagine what writing is supposed to look like. Writing should be informal at the processing stage, formal at the assessment stage.

CONTENT AREA TEACHERS AND ENGLISH TEACHERS PROBABLY HAVE DIFFERENT EXPECTATIONS

If you teach social studies or science, your expectations for writing may be more formal than the writing that the English teacher expects. We're speaking about writing for assessment now: the lab report, the position paper, the document-based essay. Likely, you want only third person point of view. You want the writer to establish an objective stance toward the subject. You want analysis and not personal reaction. You want unemotional language, heavy with content area terminology. But you don't care much about sentence variety, voice, imagery, or vivid description. We're talking about two very different genres when we compare what the content area teacher wants with what the English teacher thinks is important and spends a great deal of time on.

By saying this, I don't mean that English teachers don't value objectivity or academic language. Of course we do. Nor am I discounting the place of creative or subjective, lively writing in social studies or science. But the point is simply that content area teachers are likely to make assumptions about what has been taught, emphasized, and rewarded by English teachers. These assumptions may be the cause of mis-communications between ourselves and our students. They need to be *explicitly* taught what your expectations are. This is best done through models.

The disconnect between English class and science class, as it applies to writing expectations, grows when the science teacher "doesn't care" about grammar and "all that stuff." But the disconnect comes not only because of the non-English teacher. English teachers have the responsibility to sell students on the fact that errors in form damage the relationship between writer and reader, decreasing the power and coherence of the message. It's like driving on a smoothly-paved, well-marked road, rather than one full of potholes and signs obscured by overgrowth.

GUIDING PRINCIPLES FOR ENGLISH TEACHERS

GIVE REASONS FOR LANGUAGE EXCHANGES

When you take something away from students' language, give them something else, and give them reasons for the exchange. Unfortunately, so much of our writing instruction begins with words like "don't" and "never": *"Don't repeat yourself." "Never end a sentence with a preposition." "Don't use contractions." "Never write in the first person." "Don't split an infinitive." "Never write in the second person." "Don't begin a sentence with 'and,' 'so,' or 'but.'" "Never write a sentence fragment."* Because these "don't" and "never" admonitions are ignored in the world of professional writing, they are arbitrary injunctions that do nothing to improve writing. Not only do they do nothing to improve writing; they do actual harm to style because the cure is worse than the disease.

What's the harm? When we tell students that they can't use the first person but don't model what we want instead of it, our students tend to write in passive voice. Passive voice, though not inherently bad (no more than first person point of view is bad), should be used only for its intended purpose: to remove or delay naming the agent of the action. When writers unintentionally overuse the passive voice, the result is likely to be prose that is indirect, sluggish, even lifeless.

Many English teachers and elementary school teachers believe that the "don't" and "never" impositions prevent young writers from writing sentence fragments or from writing in an inappropriately informal style. "When they learn how to write," they say, "then they can break the rules." To me, this logic is akin to telling children that the world is flat because they wouldn't understand the world otherwise. I believe that there's a difference between teaching limited information and teaching wrong information. Limited information can be built upon when the mind is more sophisticated. Wrong information has to be un-learned. That you can't begin a sentence with "because" is wrong information.

So when you take something away from a student's lexicon, make suggestions; give reasons. Give choices. Teach evaluation of rhetoric.

- ◆ Instead of
  "Don't repeat yourself."

- ◆ Suggest
  - Repetition is absolutely necessary to make a cogent point. There's a difference between effective rhetorical repetition and filler. Use repetition to anchor key words that tell the reader your main idea.
  - Use parallel structure to express parallel ideas and structures. This will help your reader follow your ideas.

- ◆ Instead of
  "Never end a sentence with a preposition."

- ◆ Suggest
  - If you avoid ending sentences with prepositions your writing will seem stiff.
  - If you want your writing to seem more natural, end sentences with prepositions when you need to.

- ◆ Instead of
  "Don't use contractions."

- ◆ Suggest
  - Contractions give your prose a conversational, informal feel. If this is what you want, you may use contractions.
  - Some contractions, such as "n't" are considered acceptable by most readers in moderately formal writing. However, the contracted form of "have," "'ve" is often frowned upon in academic writing.

- ◆ Instead of
  "Never write in the first person."

- ◆ Suggest
  - As E. B. White advises, keep yourself in the background. Remember that you have to accommodate the writing task. If the task asks you for analysis, don't give your opinion. If the task asks for your opinion, use the first person to give it, but then switch into the third person to analyze and justify your opinion.
  - If you write in the third person, avoid the stiffness that comes from stances that refer to the generic person as "one" or "his or her." Modern stylists accept the possessive "their" to refer to collective

pronouns such as "everyone." (English-speakers have *long* accepted the match of "they" to "everyone," as in: "The teacher told everyone to leave and *they* did.")

♦ Instead of
"Don't split an infinitive."

♦ Suggest
• The so-called rule against inserting adverbs between the "to" and the verb of an infinitive phrase has long ago been disregarded as irrelevant by professional writers.
• When it comes to splitting infinitives, we advise you to boldly go where no man has gone before.

♦ Instead of
"Never write in the second person."

♦ Suggest
• Use of the second person pronoun, "you," is preferable to other syntactical choice that would result in wordiness or undue distance between the writer and the reader. The use of "one" sounds stilted and forced. Anything that sounds stilted and forced calls attention to itself, interfering with meaning.
• Avoid overuse of "you" to refer to the generic person. Say "people," "readers," "citizens." As an English teacher, you may want to spend time on this issue. In social studies, "you" might be "the citizen"; in science, "you" might be "the technician"; in art history, "you" might be "the viewer"; and in English, "you" might be "the reader."

♦ Instead of
"Don't begin a sentence with 'and,' 'so,' or 'but.'"

♦ Suggest
• Beginning a sentence with coordinating conjunctions signals a certain level of informality to some readers. If you use these conjunctions to begin a sentence in writing that is expected to be formal, you will have to compensate by using a rather formal tone elsewhere. So if you can't manage to do that, you should avoid beginning sentences with coordinating conjunctions.
• Writers begin sentences with coordinating conjunctions for two reasons. The first is to establish emphasis: the writer wants the reader to hit hard on the meaning of the conjunction so as to understand the relationship of the upcoming idea to its predecessor. The second is to establish a degree of informality.

♦ Instead of
"Never write a sentence fragment."

♦ Suggest
- Some writers use fragments deliberately, as part of their style. These writers have shown the reader that there's no doubt that they are in control of their sentence style. Having shown this, they are now free to lighten up their prose with a stylistic fragment here and there. However, stylistic fragments are a feature of moderately informal writing. In a formal research paper, only complete sentences should be used, except …
- Items in bulleted lists are usually presented as fragments. For ease of comprehension, the items in a bulleted list are best presented in parallel grammatical form.

EMPHASIZE THE IMPORTANCE OF ADJUSTING THE LANGUAGE FOR THE AUDIENCE

Instead of lamenting the lack of articulation and consistency between departments in your school, capitalize on what students can learn about how they must consider audience. As part of your writing instruction, include flexibility of diction, form, and syntax. How would the same message be worded for various audiences and contexts?

Familiarize yourself with various genres of writing that content area teachers expect. Do you know what a lab report in your school is supposed to look like? Do all science teachers in your school use a standard format? Do you know what a document-based essay is supposed to look like? Are you familiar with the kinds of constructed responses that students are expected to write for State-administered exams in other subjects? *Your* subject may be English, and your expertise and interests surely lie with literary genres; but your *students* need to know more than just literary writing to survive. Don't assume that their content area teachers are attending to this. They are assuming the same about you.

If you are fortunate enough to have conversations with your colleagues in other subject areas about what they expect in a writing task, do listen to their expectations, rather than try to change opinions. The people whose opinions are hardest to change are the very ones whose opinions you think are most outdated. By the time you "enlighten" a colleague, she will retire. Your energies are better invested in listening to what she wants, and teaching your students how to adapt, just as they will have to do in college and in the workplace. Don't lose credibility by putting your students in the middle of an interdepartmental feud.

A PARADIGM SHIFT: THE DEFICIT MODEL VS. THE RESOURCE MODEL

Teachers, especially English teachers, usually operate by a deficit model of writing instruction. By "deficit model," I mean that we are looking to find what is wrong and fix it. Although we need to point out errors and teach students to edit, a more productive way of imagining writing instruction is by thinking of writing as a resource.

Here's the difference: Teachers in the deficit model poise their red pens in the "attack" position: "Here's a mistake. I must note it." Students in the deficit model write so as to avoid these errors, often at the expense of elevated sentence structure and vocabulary. When these students get their papers back, they look at the grade, noting that a certain amount of red ink has been spilled in the generation of that grade. But teachers in the resource model look *primarily* at what the student has accomplished in terms of content. Have they used colons to present examples, reword ideas, introduce bulleted lists? Have they used lots of proper nouns and prepositional phrases to achieve specificity and detail? Students in the resource model know that if they use a semicolon to express parallel ideas they will be demonstrating an understanding of the subject. If they write with complex sentences, they can express two ideas, one of which is subordinate to the other.

The English teacher should be the one who teaches what prepositional phrases are and what they are good for. But the content area teacher can remind students that phrases beginning with *in, on, at, for,* and *with* are a good idea to use because these phrases deliver specifics. Chanting "Be specific! Be specific!" is of limited value. Giving a word bank for a given writing task is far more valuable. Include common prepositions in the word bank.

The teacher who operates from a resource model connects the upcoming writing task to subject area learning. She dishes out word lists, model sentences, outlines, and templates. But the teacher who operates from a deficit model is fearful that such assistance "gives away the store." Once we view writing as an opportunity for learning rather than as a testing situation, we become freer with positive information that will lead to durable learning in the subject area.

The terms *deficit model* and *resource model* come from psychology and social work. In the former, the clinician seeks to "fix" the family, a family that the clinician may not fully understand. In the latter, the clinician realizes that the client's family and culture are not going to go away or "be fixed" in time to help the client. The clinician looks for positive strengths upon which to build a safer environment for the client. Those educators and clinicians who have shifted to the resource model seek to nurture resilience that comes out of adversity or disability, rather than to protect "at risk" students from failure and the resilience that may come from it.

The resource model is *particularly* important with our English language learners. Here, we have the marvelous resource of another language spoken in the home and perhaps the community. To view the student's emergent fluency in English only in terms of lack of subject-verb agreement, misunderstanding of idiom, failure to conjugate verbs correctly, and skeletal sentence structure would be to inhibit the student's experimentation (growth) and miss out on the chief way of learning: prior knowledge (of the home language).

JUMPING IN

People in all walks of life are self-conscious about their writing skills. Teachers, yes even English teachers, are no exception. Many teachers are loath to include writing in their instruction because they don't feel equipped to evaluate it. Often, they have bad experiences that result from framing a task too broadly. Or, they end up with folders full of plagiarism (that they can't prove, although plagiarism is now much easier to track down, thanks to search engines and Turnitin.com). And this is not to mention the greatest damper of all: the sheer amount of time and effort that it takes to "correct" a stack of papers. Once "corrected," we then often have to justify our (already justified) grades to disgruntled students and parents. Is it worth it? Can it be any easier?

Yes to both. The former question has, I hope already been addressed and is self-evident. The latter question is the harder one to answer. Can it be any easier? Evaluating student writing *can* be easier if we learn the craft of framing the task, if we stagger due dates, if we use a rubric, if we give ourselves no more work than we can handle. At first, we underestimate the time that it will take to go through a set of papers, and we end up fearing that we will miss the end-of-quarter deadline. After several late nights and cancelled personal appointments, we get the message. We come to know just how long it will take, and we budget our time accordingly.

Sometimes, we ask for more than we need. A well-developed paragraph can be just as valuable on an in-class test as a five-paragraph essay. A bulleted list can serve the same purpose as a two-page structured report.

The National Commission on Writing in America's Schools and Colleges conducted by the College Board and published in 2003 calls for a revolution in the teaching of writing in all subject areas beginning in the earliest years of schooling.

To arm this revolution, we need ongoing staff development, administrative, and collegial support. To make writing take its rightful place as the hub of the curriculum, we're going to need training, technology, time, and personnel.

Meanwhile, let's not wait around for training, technology, time, and personnel to come along. Let's begin where we're comfortable, whether that be with lists and journals or with full-scale formal research papers. This book offers lots of valuable writing tasks for students that place reasonable, not overwhelming, demands upon teachers. Writing definitions and writing the 50-word statement are two forms that I discuss in detail. Put your words into students' mouths and hands.

BUILDING A POSITIVE CLIMATE FOR WRITING

Some students, and some teachers, are uneasy about writing. When we write, we expose not only our ideas but the ways in which we use the English language.

Not everyone is confident about their ability. Once words are committed to paper, they say something about us, or we think they do. Words on paper have a way of revealing the imperfections of their creators. No one spells every word correctly, or puts every comma in the right place, but students and teachers may feel unduly self-critical about surface mistakes. The wise teacher builds a community of learners in which the sense of being threatened is as low as possible.

Anxiety has a negative effect upon learning. Although you can't eliminate anxiety altogether, be conscious of the following anxiety-producers that being asked to write generates:

- "It has to be *how* many? I'll *never* be able to write that much!"
  Long assignments are scary. Break long assignments into manageable parts. As I've advised elsewhere in this book, assign a number of paragraphs rather than a number of words or pages.

- "I'm the world's worst speller."
  We can instruct for spelling in a productive manner that accomplishes more than just teaching letter strings. Spelling, especially of technical terms, is related to meaning, as Latin-based words have prefixes, roots, and suffixes, and each of these bears meaning. Treat misspellings clinically, looking for ways to connect words to each other to form word families. Try to find, and train students to look for, patterns. One of the strongest tenets of brain compatible learning is that the brain looks for patterns.

- "I don't want anyone to read this."
  Allow students to opt out of sharing their work with others. Ask them to read just one or two sentences, or even just a list of key words. Students do learn and establish community by reading each other's writing, but they don't have to relinquish *all* of it to the eyes of others.

- "I'll never get this done."
  Help students manage their time. Show them steps in the process. Soften your language. Instead of saying "deadline," try "finish line" or "accomplishment date." If you offer a "grace period" of five days after the due date, you give students the comforting impression that they have some latitude. Allow some of the project to be written in class.

- "All those red marks on my paper make me feel sick."
  Who ever said you had to note every error? Be stingy with the red ink, saving your corrections for real "red flag-worthy" troubles. Favor the rubric rather than the paper for negative comments. And look for the positive. You may get more attention from *one* positive and *one* negative comment on the paper than numerous corrections that the student might not even look at.

Here are some suggestions for building a positive environment that will promote writing in the content areas:

♦ **Make writing-to-learn activities routine.**
The more students write in a casual manner, the more they will build up their confidence. When students write to learn rather than to prove what they know for a grade, they build their writing skills as well as their content knowledge. Your matter-of-fact attitude that writing is part of the learning process will soften the edge of their anxiety.

♦ **Model your own writing, flaws included.**
Make your thinking visible to the students as you teach. If you use prepared overhead transparencies a lot, put some of them aside and, instead, write in real time. Make mistakes and fix them. Model the behavior of trying out different spellings and using a spelling dictionary or electronic speller if you need to.

♦ **Model enthusiasm for writing.**
Stay completely away from any negative language about writing. Talk about papers that you wrote in college that helped you learn. Act interested in what students have written.

♦ **Provide rubrics.**
Rubrics take away some of the writer's anxiety because they show exactly what is expected. A good rubric is a writer's guide. Be sure that your rubric itself does not look formidable. It should have plenty of white space.

♦ **Keep your comments supportive.**
No one likes to read that they are *wrong, wrong, wrong, bad, bad, bad.* Turn negative comments into suggestions. Keep in mind as you comment on student writing that people can improve only incrementally. Give the student one or two positive suggestions and believe in the possibility of slow and steady improvement.

♦ **Value short writing tasks.**
Whatever students write—a word, a phrase, a list, a sentence, a paragraph—is a step toward durable learning and towards building confidence and positive attitudes toward writing to learn.

♦ **Offer choice.**
Everyone feels a sense of autonomy and power when given some choice. Too much choice can be paralyzing, but if you offer two or three choices, you will get a variety of responses that students can share for more learning.

♦ **Provide access to the needed resources.**
Make Hotlists to help students find what they need. Tell students that you look to the library-media specialist to help you find resources.

♦ **Allow students to write as partners sometimes.**

Allowing students to double up cuts your work in half and can strengthen their skills. They may find out that verbalizing as they write is very helpful. This form of cooperative learning has long been used in science classes where students work with lab partners to do the experiment and write the report.

♦ **Lighten up.**

Please don't make writing a dreary task. Assert your sense of humor and light-heartedness to dream up writing experiences in which students can have fun while they learn. I believe that everyone loves language. We love to hear and use new words, play with words, write stories, be fanciful and imaginative. Think about multi-genre projects that combine words with the arts.

KNOCKING DOWN THE STUMBLING BLOCKS

Recently, I worked with a large group of teachers in a high-needs urban school district. I asked them to complete this sentence: "The biggest problem that I would have in getting my students to write is . . ." Their responses fall into three categories:

♦ "They don't think what they have to say is important."

♦ "They don't know the basics."

♦ "They are afraid to make mistakes."

These stumbling blocks amount to the same thing: students don't know where to begin writing and we don't know where to begin helping them.

The first thing to be done is to be sure that we've framed a clear and worthwhile task. We need a clear task verb, one that the students are familiar with. A school should operate from a list of task verb that are based on *Bloom's Taxonomy*. The expectations for each of the task verbs should be readily available to all students, posted on the Website, included in any daily planners or calendars that are distributed to all students.

Let's take down these stumbling blocks one at a time:

THEY DON'T THINK WHAT THEY HAVE TO SAY IS IMPORTANT

In many schools, students make the mistake of thinking that what they have to say is entirely *too* important, and we spend a lot of time getting them to withhold their opinion rather than addressing the task. However, some students come to us from cultures where students are humbled by school. These students wonder why it is they who are giving ideas and not just taking facts from a textbook or other recognized authority.

Students need to come to see writing as communication to a real person. Provide an audience. Ask students to write letters to you, answering key questions that drive the course. For example, in a social studies class, have students answer the question "Is history important to your life?" They should repeat this exercise at several strategic points in the school year, tracking the development of their relationship to the subject as they learn it and learn ways to link it to their lives.

If what our young people have to say is authentic, many people are indeed interested. Establish audience and purpose, a real context for communication.

I asked that group of teachers to brainstorm ways to remove each stumbling block. As for getting students to value their own written ideas, here are the suggestions:

- To make text-to-self connections, ask for writing that connects the content to the student's own world. Solicit responses that give new information to you as an adult who doesn't necessarily inhabit the same subculture as the student.

- Showcase student work in as many venues as possible: classroom and hallway bulletin boards, school newspaper, local newspaper, announcements over the P.A., district newsletters.

- Encourage reluctant students to read aloud one sentence of their papers. Help them to pick out a strong sentence.

- Everyone loves visible signs of success. High school students, especially those for whom school is a negative experience, are not beyond smiling when they get a sticker in their notebook!

- Remember and refer to what they've said in writing and make their comments part of your lesson.

- Invite school board members and local leaders into your classroom for town meetings.

- Initiate a voter registration drive or other worthy service project and publicize your work to the community.

- Hold school-wide or class-wide symposia on matters of social importance.

THEY DON'T KNOW THE BASICS

We can consider "the basics" as falling into two categories:

- **Writing complete sentences and building a paragraph around a topic sentence:**
  If I'm a science or a social studies teacher, I can't take time out to teach the grammatical structure of complete sentences, or paragraph development. I do have time, however, to teach students how to think about my subject in terms of complete thoughts and development from main idea to supportive details.

  - To get students past the problem of not knowing the basics of sentence and paragraph structure, I can give them templates showing the two parts of a sentence: subject and predicate. As they supply information, they are learning the basics of how to link subjects with their actions.

- A sentence, in broadest terms, comes in three patterns:
  - SOMETHING/ HAPPENS.
  - SOMETHING OR SOMEONE/ DOES SOMETHING.
  - SOMETHING OR SOMEONE/ is SOMETHING.
- With these templates, students can organize their knowledge.
- As for paragraph development, use templates and simple visual organizers to help students learn the basics of thinking in your subject.

♦ **Using the language conventions of writing:**
Students need to know how to transition from the language of speech to the language of writing. They do this on two levels: At the first level, they are learning that writing is not speech. Writing has certain characteristics, such as punctuation to mark off sentence boundaries, that speech does not have. Speech has certain elisions, such as "wanna" and "gonna" that writing does not have. If a student is accustomed to speaking a dialect such as African American Vernacular English or a strongly stylized regional dialect, they may need special instruction to help them understand the specific grammatical features that will transition them into Standard Edited Written English.

♦ In the case of African American Vernacular English, the key differentiating features are the verb *to be*, the formulation of possessives, the use of the word "go" to signify "say," and the use of the word "they" to signify "their." Many speech tendencies particularly, but not exclusively, in urban communities have features of African American Vernacular English whether or not the speakers are African American. Teaching students how to code-switch from their casual forms of speech into an academic writing style is an important way to give them basic writing skills.

♦ Beyond the basics of code-switching into "school language," students need to transition into the academic vocabulary that we expect. They need to abandon such words as "stuff," "a whole bunch," and "a lot" for words that indicate specific subject area knowledge and a serious attitude. These transitions happen over time and with explicit instruction and modeling.

THEY ARE AFRAID TO MAKE MISTAKES

♦ **They don't know the basics.**
Alternate between writing and speaking, using one to support the other.

♦ **They are afraid to make mistakes.**
  It's easy to understand this stumbling block. The solution lies largely
  in the relationship that we develop between ourselves and our students. For them to feel safe making mistakes, we need to feel comfortable with their mistakes. We need to look at their writing
  mistakes as opportunities to analyze how they think. Rather than
  slashing though mistakes with the red pen and taking points off, we
  need to approach mistakes in a way that will strengthen our communication with students. We can do that with comments such as:

  - "Help me understand what you're thinking here."

  - "Let me help you be a little more clear."

  - "Here's how you can remember to spell this word."

  - "You have part of this right. Let's see how we can fix the rest
    of it."

  - "Let's just work on one improvement at a time."

SUMMARY

Teachers who are successful in making writing a part of learning in their
subject areas take the emotional climate into account. A positive learning climate opens minds, encourages risk-taking, and creates a learning community.
In a positive learning community, students become fluent in the subject area
language.

2

FRAMING AND EVALUATING THE TASK

CHAPTER OVERVIEW

This chapter shows you how to frame a clear and meaningful writing task. We address the following questions:

♦ My students give me flat "reports" that are frequently no more than cut-and-paste jobs from the Internet. How do I *get students to move beyond "reports" and into original thinking? What do I do about the plagiarism?*

♦ I ask for a three-page report. I get half that. How do I decide *how long* a writing task should be?

♦ My students ramble and pad. How do I get them to focus on a *controlling idea* and *support?*

♦ How do I show them how to provide enough *detail?*

♦ My students use a language tone that is far too informal for academic writing. How do I get them to use the *proper terminology* of my subject area?

♦ Some of my students can do the writing assignments easily. How do I offer *challenges* for advanced students, within a given assignment?

♦ I've been teaching for a number of years, and I have a good collection of writing tasks that are coordinated to my curriculum. How do I *rework* my assignments so as to get what I want?

♦ I dread reading and grading these papers. It seems that no matter what I do, my students claim to be unpleasantly surprised by their grades. How do I *evaluate* my students' writing?

* * *

We assign a writing task with a certain assumption in our minds as to what we want. But, to our chagrin, we get responses that are vague, off-the-topic, rambling, and carelessly done.

You need to carefully and consciously frame the writing task so that the students know what to do, are prepared to do it, and know when the job is finished and whether or not they have done it well.

FRAMING THE TASK

We tell Periods 3, 5, and 8 what to do for their essay, report, or term paper and "half of them go off and do something else." Julie writes a summary when we wanted a detailed analysis; Bryant copies something right out of the encyclopedia; and Justin seems to have just taken his notes and composed them into sentences in no particular order. And almost every paper is filled with fragments, misspellings, improper documentation format, and phrasing so awkward that you need a virtual reality mask to read it.

But understand that the quality of our students' writing can be improved by a sharpening of our own question-making skills. A vague question is guaranteed to yield a disappointing response. As much as we want students to have choices in what they write, we need to frame writing tasks that are specific, substantial, and clear.

Julie, Bryant and Justin, when they are fuzzy about what's expected, activate their "automatic summary generator" or "intensive padding generator." They figure that you want "something about" the topic.

Consider the following writing assignments from a social studies teacher:

> *Assignment:* Write a _____ page report on one of the following topics. You must have at least three sources in your bibliography:
> - The Spanish Inquisition
> - The Black Plague
> - Ferdinand and Isabella
> - The Spice Trade

With directions such as this, we should be ready for shallow, broad-based "reports" in which students copy verbatim from the online encyclopedia. We won't get analysis, connections, insight, or interesting language *because we did not ask for it.*

Let's say I ask you to walk through your back yard, recording what you see. You come back with your notes and I give you a test. On the test, I ask you questions about varieties of bird life in your back yard, but your notes mention only one grayish warbler and maybe a circling vulture or two. You fail the test, obviously, because I didn't specify the expectations. This sorry circumstance happens all the time to students. They fail in the teacher's guessing game.

A well-formed question delineates the following aspects of the writing task:

- **Length** (*depth and breadth*)   ♦ **Detail** (*specifics*)
- **Focus** (*controlling idea*)   ♦ **Language tone** (*style*)
- **Task** (*key action word*)   ♦ **Terminology** (*word bank*)

A writing task should answer these essential questions:

- *What problem* am I asking students to solve?
- *What question(s)* am I asking them to answer?
- *What connections* am I asking them to make?
- *What causes and effects* am I asking them to find?
- *What conclusions and implications* am I asking them to draw?

If students have specific problems to solve, questions to answer, connections to make, causes and effects to link together, and conclusions and implications to draw, they must think critically. They can't just summarize or paraphrase. Summarizing and paraphrasing do require instruction that we address later in this book. But summarizing and paraphrasing alone do not call for higher level thinking.

LENGTH: DEPTH AND BREADTH

"How long is it supposed to be?" This is the first question students ask about a writing task. We want to answer: "As long a woman's skirt: long enough to cover what it has to, but short enough to be interesting." We give more objective parameters:

Write a three page report on . . .

Write a 500 word essay on . . .

Write a four volume treatise on . . .

But think about it; asking for a specific number of words or pages can subvert the purpose. When we require a set number of words or pages, we entice students to do two things that they love and we hate: stretch and repeat.

The Stretch and Repeat School of Writing is represented by this:

> Ferdinand and Isabella were, respectively, two monarchs in the country of Spain during the time period of the 15th (Fifteenth) Century. This time period is also known as the Age of Exploration. It is known as the Age of Exploration because many explorers went out to sea and discovered new lands. Ferdinand and Isabella were very important during the Age of Exploration. They also are considered responsible for the Inquisition. The Inquisition was a very harsh time. In this time, people who didn't believe in the Catholic religion were called heretics. Heretics were tormented very badly if they did not convert. The person in charge of the Inquisition was Tomas de Torquemada. He was Isabella's confessor.

SOCIAL STUDIES

The writer succeeds in his goal of producing 116 words in a message that could easily be expressed in less than half that. By using fewer words, but better ones, another writer packs in twice as much information.

> Ferdinand and Isabella, 15th Century monarchs of Spain, presided over the Age of Exploration as well as the Inquisition. During the Age of Exploration, Spain promoted overseas exploration by sponsoring Christopher Columbus, a Genoese adventurer. Patronage of explorers resulted in the establishment of the Spanish Empire in Peru and Mexico which would enrich the Spanish coffers with treasures of silver and gold. Ferdinand and Isabella also presided over the torment and forced conversion of heretics (non-believers of the Catholic faith). The Spanish Inquisition, as it came to be known, was headed by Isabella's confessor, Tomas de Torquemada.

If there were such a thing as "The Handbook of Padding," it would list these essentials in the art of filling up a page with the requisite number of words so that you could pursue life outside of homework:

♦ **Empty words** take up space and add no depth: *very, really, mostly, usually*

♦ **By piling on short sentences, each containing** *only one bit of information,* you can stretch out the number of words that you need to express your ideas.

♦ **Pompous phrases** such as *at the present time* and *at previous points in time* score more action wordosity points than simple, direct words such as *now* and *in the past.*

We should be after *density of information*, not length. Rather than play the word-count game, which is guaranteed to weaken writing, we suggest that you specify length in terms of *content*, not volume.

Instead of asking for a 500 word essay, ask for a four or five paragraph essay in which each paragraph is developed through *reasons, examples, facts, figures, names, places, causes, results,* and so on.

For a longer piece, instead of requiring a five to seven page paper, ask for a certain number of paragraphs and require that each paragraph contain four or five sentences each of which noticeably *adds detail and/or insight.*

The following editing activities will train students away from padded writing. The teacher might say this:

> Think of yourselves as CEOs of the Essay Corporation and that you owe it to your shareholders to reach *Maximum Word Efficiency.*

DOWNSIZING

Eliminating unnecessary words: Subject all words to scrutiny. Are they working or slacking? Fire all useless tag-along words:

With useless words: *The most recent glaciation in New York occurred so recently that this material has not weathered very extensively, and many soils in New York State are quite thin and very rocky as a result of this.*	Revised: *The last glaciation in New York occurred so recently that this material has not weathered extensively, and the soils in New York State are thin and rocky.*
Tag-along words: *As glaciers start to advance, they begin to erode all the loose soil and erode other materials from the Earth's surface and bedrock starts to be exposed.*	Revised: *As glaciers advance, they erode loose soil and other materials from the Earth's surface and expose bedrock.*

From Tarendash, A. S. 1977. *Barron's Regents Exams and Answers/Chemistry*. New York: Barron's, p. 70.

What is the difference between *beginning to erode* and *eroding? Having to measure* and *measuring? Undergoing the decaying process* and *decaying?*

SHARING OFFICE SPACE

Combining sentences: Think of each sentence as an office, and, in this company, no one has the luxury of a private office. Several key words, not just one or two, must be working in each office. Make a checkmark next to all of the "worker words" in a sentence. If a sentence has only one or two key words working in it, you must incorporate that sentence into an adjacent one.

Private Offices: *Oil is a product of decomposition. Both plant and animal remains decompose and form oil.*	Shared Space: *Oil is a product of decomposition of both plant and animal remains.*

TRAINING THE WORKFORCE

Using proper terms: Content area writing involves technical terminology, which we can think of as a trained word workforce. When we use content area terminology rather than lay terminology, we achieve conciseness.

Untrained Word Workforce: *When glaciers move forward and move backward their motions are caused by changes in the climate.*	Trained Word Workforce: *The advance and retreat of glaciers is triggered by climactic changes.*

No doubt, your students will be alarmed, not gratified, to find that they are expected to express their ideas in fewer words. To develop the piece efficiently, they will have to substitute real meaning where padding once took up space. In Chapter 3, I discuss strategies for substantiating claims and providing detail.

SUMMARY

Rethink your habit of requiring a certain number of words or pages. Such length requirements often lead to padding and poor quality writing. You can shape better writing by stipulating a given number of paragraphs and stating that each paragraph needs to contain substantial information. When you ask for a certain number of paragraphs, rather than a certain number of pages or words, you are encouraging students to think in terms of well-developed ideas rather than page-fillers. If you are an English teacher, teach paragraph shape: transition, topic sentence, support, summary and transition into the next paragraph.

FOCUS: CONTROLLING IDEA

The focus of a writing piece is also known as the *controlling idea*. There are important differences between *topic* and *focus:* Students may know the former without knowing how to do the latter. The topic can be stated as a phrase; the focus can be stated as a question. The topic suggests that information can be found in a single source; the focus may require integration from multiple sources. The topic may have a definite border; the focus may have gray areas and require the student to tolerate ambiguity. The topic consists of facts; the focus consists of facts plus interpretation.

Topic	Focus
The reign of Ferdinand and Isabella	◆ What were the *accomplishments and challenges* of Ferdinand and Isabella?
	◆ What is the *historical context* in which Ferdinand and Isabella reigned?
	◆ What are the *controversies* surrounding Ferdinand and Isabella?

The words *thesis, focus, theory,* and *ethereal* are related. These Greek words refer to something more than the literal level, something that involves lifting a topic off the page and treating it intellectually. This treatment can be stated as a question:

Topic	Focus
Glaciers	◆ What happens as glaciers retreat and advance?
	◆ What forces act upon glaciers? Why do they form and how do they change?
	◆ What effects do glaciers have on the Earth?

SOCIAL STUDIES

EARTH SCIENCE

Topic	Focus
Georgia O'Keefe	◆ What ideas and images are evoked by her subjects?
	◆ What are the similarities and differences between O'Keefe's desert paintings and her New York paintings?
	◆ What are the features of O'Keefe's paintings?
	◆ What other artists remind us of O'Keefe in style and subject?

A focus statement can be constructed as an assertion rather than as a question, but, absent a focus statement, the student is aimless and will deliver a low-level report that does not indicate engagement in the topic. The focus statement activates *thinking*.

A word about *thinking:* To "think about" something is to have it interact with something else. That is the difference between *thinking about* something and merely *picturing it*. Let's think about a swamp. We would consider its components, the creepy crawly things that slither through it. We would think about how it changes, evolves, sustains itself and all that is in it. Thinking is not just a mental image of an object or concept; it is the object or concept *in play*.

This is why we can't write anything meaningful without a focus statement. It activates thinking, as opposed to simply laying down a subject in words.

TASK: KEY WORDS AND REPETITION

Once we have a focus statement, we need to find the *key question words*. A useful source of such question words, arranged in the hierarchy of thinking levels, can be found in *Bloom's Taxonomy*. Bloom and his colleagues devised six categories of questions in ascending order of sophistication.

The chart which follows is an adaptation of *Bloom's Taxonomy* in which we've collapsed the six levels into three. Using the general topic of **the jet engine**, we've illustrated how various question words can prompt elevated thinking in a writing task.

Levels of Thinking	*Question Words*	*Writing Tasks*
Level One: Knowledge and Comprehension *You want the student to show that she recalls facts in an organized, clear sequence.*	◆ Explain in your own words identify ◆ Describe ◆ Summarize ◆ Retell ◆ Trace ◆ Ask *what?*	◆ Describe the basic workings of the jet engine. ◆ Explain in your own words how a jet engine works. ◆ List the basic parts of a jet engine and tell what these parts do. ◆ Trace the movement of air through a jet engine.

ART

PHYSICS

Levels of Thinking	Question Words	Writing Tasks
Level Two: Application and Analysis	♦ Explain how ♦ Explain why ♦ Discuss the details in relation to the whole ♦ Solve a problem by applying knowledge ♦ Explain a relationship ♦ Ask *how?*	♦ Explain the relationship between the turbofan and the compressors. ♦ Explain why the air in a jet engine has to be heated. ♦ Explain the functioning of the rotating and stationery blades in the compressors. ♦ Explain the interaction between air movement and air temperature in a jet engine.
Level Three: Synthesis and Evaluation	♦ Create ♦ Put together ♦ Suggest ♦ Judge ♦ Agree/disagree ♦ Defend/refute ♦ Prioritize ♦ Combine ideas ♦ Ask *what if? why?*	♦ Explain why a jet engine cannot work in space ♦ What would happen if the bypass duct clogged? ♦ Why is kerosene or paraffin the fuel of choice for a jet engine?

Does the writing task take the student beyond Level One thinking?

♦ **Have we asked the students to do something which cannot be simply copied out of an encyclopedia or text?**

If we've asked students to "write a report about the 1918 flu epidemic," we haven't provided enough detail. A Level Two treatment of this topic would require the student to compare the 1918 flu epidemic with the Bubonic Plague or with other influenza outbreaks. Or, the student could be asked to discuss the various lifestyle conditions (overcrowding, poverty, industrialization) that affected the high death toll.

♦ **Does the topic offer opportunities for interdisciplinary synthesis?**

We should always be thinking about how we can get students to use what they've learned in other courses. In a paper on the accomplishments of Winston Churchill, the student could bring in knowledge learned in English class about rhetorical techniques by referring to Churchill's 1938 speech in response to the Munich Agreement.

♦ **Can the student apply previous knowledge to the topic and draw conclusions, make assumptions, devise original or imaginative ideas?**

Knowledge is constructed. This means that we make meaning out of a new topic by fastening it onto the fabric of what we already know. Learning takes place when we integrate the new with the known. The following structures provide a way for students to hook new knowledge onto established knowledge, thereby making the new learning meaningful:

- *I think of . . .*

  The *I think of . . . statement* is a powerful way to connect the new to the known. It invites the student to say what something about the topic reminds him of. This opens the door to metaphorical thinking, visualization, and analogy. A student writing an essay about Ferdinand and Isabella can say *I think of the Salem witch trials, in which accused people were denied due process in a court which accepted rumor as evidence.*

- *Allow the student to make a moral judgment.*

  When we ask students to make moral judgments about historical or social issues after they've laid out the evidence, we invite them to think on the highest level. We ask them to bring the issue into the sphere of their own sense of right and wrong. In a paper about Douglas MacArthur, the student can consider the rightness or wrongness of the decision made by President Truman to fire him.

♦ **Does the topic ask the student to place the topic in its historical context?**

We can't be said to understand any serious topic unless we see where it comes from, what factors gave rise to it, how it fits into the patterns of history, and how the world changed as a result of it. A student writing about the Elizabethan Age can understand its import only if he recognizes it as a brief period of peace wedged between two tumultuous eras of civil strife in England.

♦ **Does the topic ask the student to consider the origin of key terms?**

Etymology is often the key to meaning. Much can be revealed by understanding the history of a word. A report about the nature of sedimentary rock should include the fact that the word *sediment* has *sit* at its root and is related to *sedentary, supersede, sedition, sedate, preside, president, resident,* and *subsidiary.* This will deepen his knowledge of the concept of sedimentation, and create a word web in which related words can be retained. It becomes easier to remember a meaning of a word that is associated with other words.

Note: This is not to encourage the cliché practice of opening a paper with a verbatim dictionary definition. That would be low-level thinking. Constructing a word web is higher level thinking because it takes the thinker on a word safari in search of words with similar structures.

As for repetition, consider its value in the rhetorical structure. There's good repetition and bad (like cholesterol). The good kind of repetition creates cohesion. The bad kind is just filler. Rhetorical repetition includes anchoring key words in key places, stating and then summarizing the main idea using technical language. In English class, students are encouraged to vary their vocabulary by using synonyms. But in content area writing, synonyms are not as good an idea. We want technical terms, and there are no synonyms for these. Among the "rethinkings" that you might be doing about your advice to students about writing, you might want to rethink what you tell them about avoiding repetition.

DETAIL: SPECIFICS

A writing task should have numbers in it:

♦ Give *two* reasons

♦ Give *three* specific examples

♦ Identify *four* types of . . .

♦ Explain *five* different ways to . . .

We always require that students be specific. How exactly do they get there? They need all or some of the following: *facts and figures, quotations, visuals.*

FACTS AND FIGURES

Facts and figures come in the form of proper nouns and numbers:

♦ Names

♦ Dates

♦ Places

♦ Statistics

♦ Technical terms

> *Assignment:* Compare the 1918 flu epidemic to the Black Death of the Thirteenth Century. Discuss at least three aspects of these plagues, such as the nature of the virus, how it spread, and the role played by living conditions.

For this topic, the student would have to:

♦ Use the technical terminology regarding viruses and disease

♦ Refer to cities and countries

♦ Refer to dates

♦ Describe aspects of crowded and unhygienic living conditions of the two periods

SOCIAL STUDIES/ BIOLOGY

QUOTATIONS

These could be quotations spoken by the person who is the subject of the report, by a witness to an event, or by an established expert. The quotation should lend itself to interpretation, to an *in other words statement:*

> Winston Churchill, in response to the Munich Agreement of 1938, said: *We are now in the presence of a disaster of the first magnitude.* In other words, the Third Reich had now passed the point of no return and there was no avoiding the catastrophes looming ahead.

VISUALS: THE PICTURE . . . STATEMENT

The more abstract the concept, the more necessary it is to provide a visual image. This image can be literal or metaphorical. The mathematical theory known as *six degrees of separation* is a concept that is inaccessible without a picture to go with it:

> The smallness of a world or network can be expressed mathematically by the number of steps it takes to get from one element of it to any other. This depends on the degree of regularity of a network's interconnections. (Blakeslee, S. "Mathematicians Prove that It's a Small World." *New York Times*. 16 June 1998.)

To make this concept accessible with a picture statement, we could say:

> Picture two concentric circles with twenty points evenly spaced on the outer circle. When we connect adjacent points, we are not bisecting the circles, but when we bisect the circles, we create more points of contact. Picture a shortcut across any system, such as electric power grids, the Internet, or the lines along which rumors spread. The rumor passed from neighbor to neighbor reaches fewer points than the tale that travels across town, there to be disseminated across a wider network, making the world smaller.

MATH

LANGUAGE TONE: STYLE

One of our biggest complaints about student writing is that the word choice is too casual. As teachers of social studies, art, science, mathematics, etc., we present an array of specialized language which differs from lay terminology. The essence of learning our subject is learning to use its language. A student comparing the symbolic art of Keith Haring to ancient Greek vases might say:

> *Keith Haring painted things like dancing figures and barking dogs. These things are also on the ancient Greek vases that Keith would see in the museums in New York.. Keith was like an artist of people on the streets. He did paintings on playground walls in the streets like Crack is Wack.*

ART

Although this student knows exactly what she's talking about, she loses credibility because her tone is too conversational. To ask for acceptable language tone, we should ask the student to dress up the words for the occasion: "These are *working words*, not *at-home* words." Students understand and accept the social conventions of dress, especially if we give them the examples of hospital personnel: "How can you tell who the doctors and nurses are? When you go into Home Depot, how can you tell the shoppers from the workers?"

Words such as *things, like,* or *stuff* are not dressed for lab work. Similarly, we don't refer to the artist by his first name, even if his work appeals to us on a personal level.

When we ask the writer of the Keith Haring statement what the *things* are, she will say: *images, pictures, symbols*. With these words, she can be specific as well as appropriate, which is what proper language tone is all about.

Style refers to word choice, sentence structure, and an elusive quality called *voice*. A writer needs to adjust her voice to the particular situation, developing a repertoire of language styles.

TERMINOLOGY: WORD BANK

Each content area has an inventory of words that suits its language tone. Part of the purpose of content area writing is to have the student *talk the talk:* learn the lexicon of biology, history, economics, mathematics, etc.

Giving students a word bank of ten to fifteen terms suited to the topic goes a long way toward getting them to use the proper terminology and to focus on specifics. But students often avoid technical terminology because of spelling. The way the English language works is that the more specific a word is, the more it tends to have a Greek or Latin word base, and that plays out in words that are long and scary.

For the Keith Haring piece, in explaining the influence of Haring's street murals to ancient Greek vases, the student could have worked from a word bank consisting of the following terms:

energy lines	negative image	radiating lines
geometric shapes	organic shapes	random patterns
mirror images	positive space	texture
mural		

Word banks used as a prewriting strategy address specificity, proper language tone, spelling, and substance.

CHALLENGE: CONSIDER

Finally, we can hone the writing task even further by giving a *Challenge: Consider* statement: To *consider* is to *sit with*. The *Challenge: Consider* statement directs the student to higher level thinking.

♦ Explain the basic principles of the six degrees of separation theory. Give three examples of how this theory applies to the relationships that people have because of technologies.

Challenge: Consider the differences between communication technology now as compared to fifty years ago.

♦ Explain how and why acid rain effects aquatic plant life.

Challenge: Consider how these effects upon aquatic plant life effect at least three species.

SUMMARY

A well-constructed writing task suggests a length based on the number of well-developed paragraphs rather than on a certain number of words or pages. The writing task features an active word (e.g., *describe, analyze, explain, discuss, enumerate, show*) that places the student in lower, middle, or higher level thinking. That active word must have an object (*describe the effects of, analyze the workings of, explain the reasons for, discuss the results of, enumerate the types of, show the relationship of*). The task should stipulate the number of reasons, examples, results, types that are expected. (*Scholastic Art.* April/May 1998, 16.)

SAMPLE WRITING TASKS: LEAKY AND AIRTIGHT

What follows are examples of leaky writing tasks and how they can be made airtight. Some of these topics are specific, and you may not want every student in the class writing about the same subject. In these cases, we've extrapolated the particular subject to a broader one, to allow for student choice and variety.

LEVEL ONE THINKING

♦ **Leaky:** Write a two page report, double-spaced, describing the spice trade routes and their influence on the Age of Exploration. Use at least two sources.

• **Leaks:** If all that is required is a description of the spice trade routes, the student might just as well draw (or copy) a map of them. As for the influence of the spice trades on the Age of Exploration, does the teacher want to know *why* spices were important in European life *or* is she asking about the international competition to find an overland route to India? Is the student supposed to discuss *how* the spice trade resulted in intercultural exchanges of ideas? As for the sources, is a map of the spice trade routes considered one source?

♦ **Airtight:** The spice trade routes played an important part in the Age of Exploration. Copy a map of the spice trade routes and explain at least two of them in your own words. Each route should be explained in one paragraph. Your explanations should include at least four geographic features (e.g., *mountains, bodies of water, deserts*) and an explanation of how these features influenced the decisions of the travelers. In one paragraph, tell the importance of spices during the Fifteenth Century. Give specific examples of at least two spices and tell what these were used for.

Challenge: Consider the unexpected dangers that lay in wait on these routes. (At least three paragraphs, plus introduction and conclusion.)

♦ **Extrapolation:** Routes have played significant roles throughout history. Select a particular era in history in which routes were sought and traveled. Find (set number of) maps which illustrate (set number of) routes . . .

At this point, the essay can follow the pattern of the above essay. This essay has two parts. The first is to have the student show how a route follows particular geographic features. The second is the significance of the goal of the route itself: in this case, spices. This topic can be extrapolated to any route that was established for a commercial product and the need for that product. It could also be expanded to include routes for religious and political purposes. The idea is to have students find routes on a map, refer to geographic features that determine the route, and explain why there was a need for whatever it was that brought about travel along this route.

♦ **Leaky:** Write a two page, double-spaced report explaining how an internal combustion engine works. Include a hand-drawn illustration labeling the main parts.

  • **Leaks:** This report can be easily copied. The labeled illustration is a good idea, and can be used to form the basis of a report that is more likely to be written in the student's own words.

♦ **Airtight:** You are baby-sitting for your friend's younger brother who is in the fourth grade. He looks over your shoulder as you answer questions in the text about the workings of the internal combustion engine. Write a Q & A script in which you explain how the engine works. Assume that your young student will want you to explain technical terms in simpler language.

Challenge: Consider helping him to learn the technical terms by linking them to items in his room. (At least ten questions and answers.)

♦ **Extrapolation:** Explain the workings of a complicated system to a person who needs an explanation in simple, straightforward language. Use Q & A form.

PHYSICS

- **Leaky:** Watch the movie *Amadeus* and write a three page report which summarizes the life of Wolfgang Amadeus Mozart. Use one other source about Mozart.
  - **Leaks:** The student is likely to launch into a summary of the movie in the *then, then, and then* style. The "other source" may not add any insight above and beyond the movie.

- **Airtight:** Watch the movie *Amadeus* and discuss Mozart's challenges and choices. Describe three different challenges and three different choices in one paragraph each. Develop each paragraph by referring to specific scenes. Be sure to note names, dates, and places as you watch the film.

  Challenge: Consider what the effects on Mozart's music would have been had he made other choices.

- **Extrapolation:** Watch or read a biography, and describe three challenges or choices faced by the person.

- **Leaky:** Write a five page report about the Cathedral of Notre Dame. Use three sources.
  - **Leaks:** Not only can this topic be easily copied, but the student is invited to ramble. Because the Cathedral is visual, there should be some use of illustrations, but the task does not say anything about how to use these.

- **Airtight:** Consult at least three illustrated books on the Cathedral of Notre Dame and other Gothic cathedrals. Imagine that you are visiting the Cathedral as part of your trip to Paris, and write a detailed description for your travel journal of at least two angles of the outside and at least three areas on the inside. Be sure to use proper architectural terminology, and include a glossary of at least ten terms. Your report should include at least five hand-drawn or copied illustrations with original captions beneath each.

  Challenge: Consider presenting the illustrations as post cards that you are sending to friends at home. Describe the picture on each post card in at least two sentences. The purpose of the post cards is to show off your knowledge of architecture and art.

- **Extrapolation:** In your travel journal, write a detailed description of a historically significant building.

MUSIC

SOCIAL STUDIES/ART

♦ **Leaky:** Write an essay about a person in history or someone you know who has overcome obstacles to follow a dream or fulfill an ambition.

In your article, be sure to include:

- Who the person is
- What he or she did
- The challenges he or she faced
- How the challenges were overcome
- An introduction, a body, and a conclusion

• **Leaks:** This essay is taken from the English Language Arts Test Sampler Draft and was administered to all Grade 8 students in New York State. Although there are no length specifications, the model paper looks like a typical 200-word, three-paragraph report about baseball pitcher Jim Abbot. Although Jim Abbot is a good choice, this type of topic can often yield treacly reports about relatives and friends, real or imagined, who suffered all manner of illness and disaster. Often, the writer descends into sentimentality about the loved one's courage in the face of illness, and the teacher finds herself in the awkward position of downgrading a paper that expressed heartfelt emotions about a student's real life. To avoid this uncomfortable dilemma, we are better off sticking to well-known people, unless we are looking for an essay based on personal experience. Because this is an on-demand task, the information can't be copied, but the requirements miss the opportunity to engage the student in higher level thinking.

The question is flawed in that it uses inconsistent terminology, referring to the task first as an *essay*, then as an *article*. These terms are not synonymous. An essay has a drier tone than an article. We assume that the term *article* refers to the type of feature article that would use catchy, upbeat language, unlike an essay, which would be straightforward and factual in tone. To be even more persnickety, we could say that Jim Abbot, being alive and well, is not yet a part of history. This may seem like too fine a point, but, on a formal state examination in writing, many students will take the question literally, and they have every right to do so.

Not only that, but writing about a historical figure is not an interchangeable task with writing about a person you know. The assumptions are not the same: the reader is assumed to have a certain knowledge base about the historical figure that she is not expected to have about the real person in the writer's life. The reader can't check the accuracy of facts about a the writer's next door neighbor or Aunt Shirley.

♦ **Airtight:** Write a three paragraph essay about a person in history, or in popular culture, who has overcome obstacles to follow a dream or fulfill an ambition.

In your essay, be sure to include

- A brief description of the person's role in history, or popular culture
- His or her major accomplishments
- The challenges that he or she faced
- How the challenges were overcome

Be sure that the person whom you choose achieved his dream or ambition by overcoming specific challenges.

Challenge: Consider how one type of challenge, such as a physical handicap, can lead to other challenges, such as economic hardship or lack of social acceptance.

LEVEL TWO THINKING

- ♦ Explain *how*
- ♦ Explain *why*
- ♦ Discuss *the details in relation* to the whole
- ♦ Solve a problem by *applying knowledge*
- ♦ Explain a *relationship*
- ♦ *Compare*

LEVEL TWO TOPICS

- ♦ **Leaky:** Explain the workings of one of the following systems: a nuclear reactor, municipal government in a large city, a symphonic orchestra, a major department store chain, or the circulatory system.

  - **Leaks:** This is an interesting writing task that has much potential for high-level thinking about relationships of parts to the whole in a complex system. As is, it misses the opportunity to have the students choose a complex system and write a proposal explaining their choice.

    To begin with, we can seize the teachable moment to define what we mean by a complex system and to generate multiple examples from various fields: What is a system? How do we distinguish between a simple system and a complex system? As you go about your school day, what complex systems are part of each of your subject areas? How are these systems organized in terms of purpose, leadership, structure, and parts?

INTERDISCI-
PLINARY

♦ **Airtight:** Explain the workings of any complex system. Begin by defining what a complex system is, and identify the system that you have chosen for your report. Develop your report by explaining each of the following in one or more paragraphs: purpose, leadership, structure, and parts. Be sure to explain how the parts relate to the whole, to the leadership, and to each other in the functioning of the system. Write a one paragraph proposal for your paper in which you explain why you chose this particular system and provide a general overview (one or two sentences) describing the system.

Challenge: Consider a possibility: How might it be possible for this system to be adapted to another use? made more efficient? made more reliable?

♦ **Leaky:** Discuss the contributions of a historical figure who had an impact on society in the United States in the period between the Civil War and World War I. Your report should be two to three pages in length.

  • **Leaks:** The teacher here is missing the opportunity to have students consider the ambiguities of history. The period in question is replete with robber barons, captains of industry who advanced American society with blood on their hands.

♦ **Airtight:** Analyze one positive and one negative aspect of the accomplishments of a controversial historical figure in the period between the Civil War and World War I. A controversial person is someone who is positive to some, negative to others. Your analysis should include an overall summary of the person's accomplishments, the characteristics of the time, the place in which the person had influence, and specific examples of positive and negative accomplishments. What types of people *benefited* from this person's accomplishments, and what types of people *suffered* because of them? What is the nature of the benefits or sufferings? Focus on the person's professional life, not his or her personal life. Your report should have at least ten paragraphs.

Challenge: Consider a person in the current decade who has affected society in both positive and negative ways.

♦ **Leaky:** Compare two jazz musicians. Two pages.

  • Leaks: Are the students supposed to discuss their personal lives? choice of music? venues? interpretations? range? influence? This leaky assignment represents the typical flaw of asking students to do too much in too little space. Also, according to these directions, the student could choose two jazz musicians who are vastly different, making the task of comparing them too easy. The more

SOCIAL STUDIES

MUSIC

similar two fields are, the more intellectual brainpower must be applied in comparing them.

♦ **Airtight:** Select two jazz musicians who are similar in any of the following variables: style, showmanship, venue, emotionality, rhythm, repertoire, instrumentation, genre, or time/place. Compare these two musicians on several of these variables, giving specific examples. Your report should be at least six paragraphs long.

Challenge: Consider the same song as interpreted by both musicians. Your report must use musical terminology and must place these musicians in a historical context. Discuss their influence on the music world as well as the other musicians who influenced them.

♦ **Leaky:** Write a two page report about one year in the Twentieth Century.

  • **Leaks:** If all we want is a recitation of events that occurred in a particular year, we should ask for a time line, not a written report. But we can bring this up to Level Two thinking if we ask for a relationship between the particular year and its historical context. Why did a given event occur at that particular time? What happened in subsequent years that resulted from it?

♦ **Airtight:** Write a report about three key events that occurred in a particular year of the Twentieth Century. One event would be something that is widely known as happening on a particular date, having clear historical consequences, such as the beginning of a war or an assassination. The other event should be less known, but an important result of previous events or a cause of future events, such as a Supreme Court decision. The third event should be something unpredictable or unexpected, such as a disaster or surprising pop cultural event, such as the arrival in the United States of the Beatles in 1964 or of an influential person. You may choose your event(s) from the following fields: international relations, economics, law, science/technology, the arts, sports and entertainment, lifestyles, or nature. In addition, include a timeline of major events of that year. Develop this report in twelve paragraphs.

Challenge: Consider how we view this event from various perspectives today, as compared with how it was viewed (from various perspectives) at the time.

INTERDIS-CIPLINARY

LEVEL THREE TOPICS

♦ **Leaky:** Write a ten page research paper on cloning which describes the process. Do you think humans will ever be cloned? If so, make a prediction as to when this will happen and what the advantages or disadvantages will be.

- **Leaks:** Cloning, being a monumental topic of epic proportions, qualifies as one of the best topics we can ask students to learn about and reflect upon. Asking the student to make an evaluation is higher order thinking, but, as phrased here, the evaluation is too broad, allowing the student to look down the slippery slope without having to actually negotiate it, stone by treacherous stone.

♦ **Airtight:** Write a researched position paper of at least twenty-five paragraphs which discusses the process and ethical dilemmas of cloning. Approximately 20% of your report should describe the process and give some background of the technology of cloning. In the remaining 80%, pose at least three specific cases in which cloning would be morally acceptable *or* unacceptable to you. Your paper will be interesting to the extent that your examples are realistic, well-developed, and morally vexing. An obvious moral violation, such as cloning people in order to sell their body parts on the open market, is not as interesting as a case in which a childless couple would use cloning as a way of parenting a wanted child.

Challenge: Consider how economics plays a role in the moral dilemmas of cloning.

♦ **Leaky:** Write a 1,000-word position paper about animal rights. Give reasons for your opinions.

- **Leaks:** This is a substantial, researchable, appropriate topic, but it needs to be subdivided and focused. As it is, it leads the student down the path of least resistance. A student can avoid hard moral dilemmas by making the obvious case that people should not warehouse animals in filthy conditions, depriving them of basic needs, nor should they amuse themselves by torturing animals or using them for frivolous and fruitless experimentation without anesthesia. In order to salvage this worthy topic, the teacher needs to direct the student into the gray area, where his moral antennae and intellectual lights, based on research, will guide him. This is a good topic for evaluating the validity of research sources. Animal rights groups and their opponents in industry provide much literature, and not all of it is creditable. The evaluation of source validity is at the highest level of critical thinking.

♦ **Airtight:** Select one of the following areas of animal rights and write a position paper of eight to ten paragraphs. Support your facts and figures with research from a variety of sources, including disinterested (neutral) institutions as well as animal rights advocates and those with a commercial interest:

- Animal rights regarding medical experimentation and research
- Animal rights regarding the cosmetics industry
- Protection of endangered species
- Animal rights regarding the food industry
- Animal rights vs. the rights of the pet industry<end bullets>

In your position paper, begin with an *arguable thesis statement*. State the issue(s) of controversy and who the stakeholders are. If there are advocacy groups speaking for this issue, state who they are and their agendas. State your position clearly and support it with facts and figures taken from a variety of sources, specific examples, analogies, historical background, and projections for the future.

Challenge: Consider making your opinion publicly known by writing letters to the editor and/or to public officials

♦ **Leaky:** Write a position paper of two pages in which you nominate a person for the Peace Prize of the Twentieth Century.

- **Leaks:** The teacher has posed a thoughtful question but has trivialized it by couching it in terms of a contest. Doing so reduces profound accomplishments to so many quantifiable units to be tallied up and compared. A more sober approach would allow for ambiguities.

♦ **Airtight:** The United Nations is sponsoring an essay contest among high school students. The topic is Peacemakers of the Twentieth Century. You are invited to propose a person to be named as one of ten Peacemakers of the Twentieth Century who will have their pictures displayed in a prominent place in the Secretariat. You should establish criteria for the Peacemakers, and then show by specific example how your nominee meets these criteria. Entries should be no more than six to eight paragraphs.

Challenge: Consider the role played by technology in establishing peace.

CONNECTIONS

The following chart shows how various topics can be extended and refined by making connections to other disciplines.

ART

BIOLOGY

Topics/ Connections	Interdis- ciplinary Synthesis	Historical Context	Prior Knowledge	Word Origins
Compare the art of Keith Haring to the art found on ancient Greek vases.	Combines knowledge of art with knowledge of ancient Greek culture and symbolism.	Research the genre of street art and pop art in terms of its history, conventions, and key figures.	List the various forms of street art and pop culture art that you've seen in the past month.	How does the etymology of the following words broaden your understanding of their meanings? What other words are related to the following? ◆ Symbol ◆ Graffiti ◆ Mural
Discuss the status of a particular endangered species.	Combines knowledge of mathematics, environmental science, biology, and anthropology.	What other species have become extinct? What has been the eco- logical impact of other extinctions? What species have been removed from the endangered species list? How were they able to replenish their numbers?	Discuss the relationships that you know exist among species.	Animal names are a fascinating aspect of language. Look up the etymology of several animals with funny or exotic names and explain how these names came into the English language. What do we learn about the animal by learning the history of its name? (e.g., *Platypus* means *flat face.*)

Framing and Evaluating the Task

Topics/ Connections	Interdis- ciplinary Synthesis	Historical Context	Prior Knowledge	Word Origins
Trace the history of jazz in terms of the Mississippi River.	Combines knowledge of geography, history of slavery, and musicology.	How is jazz related to African music? What other forms of music have been influenced by jazz?	Give several examples of different types of jazz.	Look up the etymology of the word jazz. How does the history of this word give us insight into the impact of the music upon our psyches?
Describe the technology of claymation.	Combines knowledge of art, technology, and literary interpretation.	What was the earliest form of claymation? Compare it to modern claymation.	Give several examples of claymation that you've seen.	Claymation is animation using clay figures. What other types of ani- mation are there? Make a list of words that refer to various types of animation.

When we see that a topic is rich enough to be distributed across this chart, then we know that this will be a thinking task, not just a copy job.

THE STATEMENT OF INTENT (PREWRITING REFLECTION)

For higher-order thinking tasks, it's a good idea for the student to reflect on what she is expected to do *before getting started*. This differs from the dreaded *in this paper I am going to . . .* statement because the statement of intent will not be an actual part of the paper. In it, the student lays out what she is expected to do. It is for the student's own use, to serve as a checkpoint of communication be- tween teacher and student.

♦ *I'm expected to explain the difference between nuclear fission and nuclear fusion and give one example of each. I need to provide visuals for fission and fusion.*

♦ *I'm expected to describe four key aspects of Gothic architecture and explain the purpose of each of these. I'll talk about gargoyles (drainage), flying
buttresses (support for high windows, high arches (visual impact and
acoustics), and stained glass (beauty and religious inspiration).*

The student can use the statement of intent in various ways:

♦ As a checkpoint between teacher and student so that the teacher can
see that the paper is grounded.

♦ As a way to formulate a thesis statement to introduce the paper.

♦ As the center of a concept map (idea web) or outline.

EVALUATING THE WRITING TASK

I decided to include information about evaluating writing tasks in this chapter about framing the task because you really need to think about both together.
As you think about what you want and how you are going to explain the directions to students, you need to let them know how the task is going to be
evaluated.

Although English teachers tend to be more at ease with evaluating student
writing tasks than do content area teachers, even English teachers will admit
that assigning scores to papers is problematical as well as tedious. To help you
become more effective and efficient at processing a set of papers, I offer information about some aids to evaluation:

♦ Rubrics and scoring guides   ♦ Self-reflective assessment

♦ Holistic scoring   ♦ Prescriptive evaluation

♦ Selected-trait scoring

RUBRICS AND SCORING GUIDES

The term *rubric* has been a fixture in the educational lexicon since the late
1990s. Actually, a rubric is just another word for *scoring guide*. Teachers have
become accustomed to creating these scoring guides. Indeed, most teachers
are expected to rely on them to justify the grades that they assign to student
writing.

A rubric (scoring guide) is a clear delineation of the traits that the teacher
considers important. The rubric has a continuum to indicate the extent to which
the writer has achieved mastery on each of the traits. Most rubrics appear in
the form of a chart upon which the teacher checks the squares that indicate the
level of mastery. The traits are listed along the vertical axis; the continuum for
mastery is on the horizontal. Some teachers prefer rubrics that list just the traits
down the page, with the numbers 1-4 or 1-6, indicating the extent of mastery for
each trait.

If a rubric is too specific, it will turn into a recipe. If that happens, the student isn't being asked to do enough original thinking. If a rubric is too general, it won't form a useful guide to the student, nor will it communicate valuable information about the student's extent of mastery on discrete traits.

Rubrics should be predictable and consistent. State examinations offer rubrics, and localities should adopt some version of them. Many rubrics provided by state education departments are too verbose for students to use, but they can be simplified.

The wording on the rubric has to be flexible enough to accommodate the various strengths and weaknesses that students will demonstrate. Some teachers like to leave space on the rubric to reward or deduct points for unexpected offerings. Some teachers weight the traits on the rubric; others give each trait equal weight.

I've settled upon "Addressing the Task" as the Number One Trait on my rubrics, both for my own English classes and the classes of the content area teachers with whom I work. Over and over again, I find that students' greatest downfall is that they have skirted the question. And once they've done that, their papers are unsatisfactory regardless of what other traits they may have done well.

After "Addressing the Task," the most prominent trait is "Development." A paper is well developed if it asserts a main idea and offers support. The support can come as examples, reasons, explanations, descriptions, quotations, evidence, statistics, and proper nouns. Many struggling writers just can't think of enough support to flesh out their paper. We can help students develop their papers by framing the task in such a way that they can draw information from its wording. Development is aided by the next two traits on my rubric, which are "Organization" and "Language."

The third trait on my rubric is "Organization." Organization is about structure: an introduction that shows that the writer understands the task and is establishing expectations for the reader. In an expository essay, we expect a thesis statement. An organized paper links one paragraph to the next and links one sentence to the next. Anything that is organized—an event, an album, an essay—has form. Forms have recognizable features that appear in predictable places. Anything that is organized has centrality: all of its pieces feed into a main idea.

Fourth is "Language." English teachers may include syntax in this trait; content area teachers usually don't. Content area teachers are interested in proper use of terminology as well as a serious academic language tone. Thus, for content area teachers, "Language" has two parts, the first of which has to do with technical terminology; the second, general diction, conveys a serious attitude toward the subject and task.

Finally, I have space for English skills: grammar, spelling, punctuation, capitalization (GSPC).

ALL-PURPOSE WRITING RUBRIC (SCORING GUIDE)

Addressing	Excellent	Good	Satisfactory	Unsatisfactory
The Task Showing a clear and consistent understanding of what the directions are asking you to do.				
Development Showing a clear main idea and supportive information				
Organization Showing strong structure, with introduction, well-developed paragraphs, conclusion, and transitions. Visual features of text assist the reader.				
Language Showing under-standing of and flexibility with the special lan-guage of the sub-ject; using proper academic diction				
GSPC Showing consis-tent care in gram-mar, spelling, punctuation, and capitalization				

HOLISTIC SCORING AND GROUP GRADING

Holistic scoring is a mindset for evaluating writing that places great value upon the immediate impression that the reader gets about the piece. Holistic scorers read for overall understanding and competencies, the way one would read authentic written material. Holistic scoring is generally used for summative, as opposed to formative, assessments. Such is the case because with a summative task, a final examination or a state-sponsored test, the students are not going to receive constructive itemized feedback. They receive grades only.

Aside from summative assessments, teachers might score holistically for in-class (on-demand) writing. We don't expect such writing to be polished. The students have time for only a best-effort first draft under time constraints.

What is the place of a rubric in holistic scoring? Holistic scorers do use a rubric to inform their evaluation, but not in the trait-by-trait manner that they would use if they were planning to return the paper to the students with constructive commentary. The rubric serves to standardize the expectations for multiple scorers who read anchor papers and discuss them in terms of the rubric before they grade papers independently. Holistic scorers are expected to know the rubric extremely well, well enough to function without looking at it as they evaluate papers.

It's very important that the group of scorers take the time to discuss the anchor papers. The goal of these collegial discussions is for the group to establish what it means to conform to the anchor papers. Teachers operating in this model should seek to understand how the anchor papers comport with the rubric.

We think in terms of broadly delineated scores when we score holistically. The New York State English Language Arts Exams (fourth and fifth grade levels) are scored on a 1-4 scale, with no fractions (*English Language Arts Test Sampler Draft*. 1998. CTB/McGraw Hill, p. T-35). The Advanced Placement exams in English and social studies rate essays on a 1-9 scale. Some people prefer an even number of calibrations. This is to force a choice between the positive or negative side. (The belief is scorers would be too tempted to settle on a middle score if there are odd numbers.)

SELECTED-TRAIT SCORING

Selected-trait scoring is a system that evaluates a limited number of the traits on the rubric. This kind of scoring is most likely to be used by English teachers, but content area teachers certainly may want to focus on one or two traits to the exclusion of others. They may want to grade a task only on its support for main ideas, or use of language, or organization.

The justification for selected-trait scoring is that you want students to concentrate on, and thus improve, certain areas of writing. On the downside, once you let students know that English usage and spelling don't count, or that organization is not a factor, you could be inadvertently making your job more frustrating. To avoid this, you could always work up a mathematical formula that magnifies certain traits while diminishing others.

I would caution any teacher against saying that "anything goes" in terms of English usage and spelling. Learning how to spell a word can give insight into that word's family. We use etymology (a word's family tree) to connect spelling to meaning. So we should exploit the learning opportunities that lie waiting to be discovered in spelling.

I would also caution against discounting the use of academic diction. Not only does accurate diction facilitate understandings between student and teacher, but the very act of having to speak in a serious tone of voice on paper makes students take the task more seriously.

Like holistic scoring, selected-trait scoring can work for in-class writing, where the student has not had time to revise. The teacher might say, "I'm looking for cause-effect statements," or "I'm not looking for transitions this time." It's possible that by *not* paying attention to certain traits of good writing this time, the student will consciously pay *more* attention to them when full-trait grading is in effect.

SELF-REFLECTIVE ASSESSMENT

Some teachers find that it works well to occasionally ask students to write reflective and goal-setting statements to improve their own writing. Students use a rubric to show where they think they fall on the given traits and then map out their own improvement plans. Some teachers use simple checklists generated from the rubric to show progress and goals. Students can transform a rough draft into a final paper this way.

SOME SENTENCE STEMS FOR SELF-REFLECTIVE ASSESSMENT

♦ I need to say more about_____because
  • I haven't made myself clear.
  • I'm making a convincing point, and I should stay with it more
  • I haven't developed this paper enough.

♦ I need more (examples, reasons, facts)_____because
  • I'm making too many assumptions.
  • Examples, reasons, and facts would support my main idea
  • I've gone off topic.
  • My paper is disorganized.

♦ I need to check_____because
  • I could have some serious misspellings.
  • My facts could be wrong.
  • I'm not sure this is what I was supposed to do.
  • I'm not sure how long this was supposed to be.

♦ I need to be clearer about_____because
  • My words are too general.
  • I haven't set forth a definite opinion.
  • I seem to be contradicting myself.
  • I haven't specified how I am using a key term.

♦ I need to delete_____ because
  • I've already said it.
  • It's filler.
  • I can't support it.
  • It is not clear.

PRESCRIPTIVE EVALUATION

Prescriptive evaluation is formative evaluation that views the student's work diagnostically. The teacher says: "What does this student need to learn *first* to move to the next level on one trait of the rubric?" With prescriptive evaluation, students are not finished when the grade is on the paper. In fact, teachers may not even grade the paper until the student satisfies given requirements (prescriptions). The prescriptions may look like this:

♦ Clarify, in writing, what this question is asking you to do.

♦ Make an outline.

♦ Make an organizational diagram.

♦ Make a vocabulary list for this writing task.

♦ List evidence that supports your main point.

The above prescriptions are content-based. English teachers may add style-based prescriptions, directing students to certain lessons to improve grammar, spelling, punctuation, and capitalization.

The paperwork for prescriptive evaluation can get out of control. To manage the paperwork and record-keeping, I suggest centralizing a set of generic lessons on a class or school Website.

I have my own class Website through Myschoolonline:

  http://myschoolonline.com/site/0,1876,5813-154891-4-33049,00.html.

Through this Website, I refer students to various lessons that address demonstrated needs that I note as I read essays. If my students want to work on their skills on their own, they can do the lessons in the "Step Up on the Rubric" folder. Some of these lessons are links to reinforcers of skills that I found on the Internet; but most of them are lessons that I wrote myself. These lessons are an extension of my classroom voice.

Hendrick Hudson High School, the high school where I teach, has a link on its Welcome Page that we call RxWrite:

  http://www2.lhric.org/henhud/rxwrite/home.htm.

RxWrite is a collection of lessons that teachers in all subjects can use to improve demonstrated needs in student writing. Teachers refer their students to RxWrite lessons for differentiated instruction.

The Freehold Regional High School District maintains a district-wide website in which lessons are keyed to the New Jersey State English Language Arts standards in both reading and writing.

Prescriptive lessons, although they take some time to set up, are a great way to follow through on written tasks that still need work. They can be used not only for remediation, but for advancement as well.

COPING WITH THE PAPERWORK LOAD

Processing student writing is demanding and time-consuming. If you find it overwhelming, you might not continue this valuable practice. The following are some suggestions to keep the volume of paperwork from getting the best of you:

♦ Don't feel that you have to read and respond to *everything* that students write. You certainly don't have to micromanage writing-to-learn activities. In fact, doing so is counterproductive, as students need the freedom to express questions and points of clarification without your oversight. Even when students write formal essays, there's no law that requires you to grade every single one. You can ask students to hand in their best of several (after checking that they've done them all).

♦ Don't feel compelled to "correct" every error. Decide to make one or two corrections on each paper, but hold students accountable to improve their skills. Have them keep their own tracking sheets where they record your comments. Periodically, they should hand in a summary report of these comments.

♦ Emphasize components. Evaluate only the thesis statements or only the supportive examples every once in a while.

♦ Vary the kinds of writing that you assign. Not everything has to be written in the form of an essay. Essays are the hardest genre to read (except maybe creative writing, which is very difficult to evaluate). Assign lists, outlines, labeled diagrams, definitions, and short statements.

♦ Accept student writing by e-mail or on disk. You may find on-screen writing easier to handle than writing on paper. You can use the "comment" feature from the Insert menu. You can even use the "Auto Correct" feature to insert prepared comments and assign students to prescriptive lessons.

STUDENT-TEACHER-TASK: GOOD TO GO

If you have framed your task effectively, and if you've thought about and communicated how you are going to evaluate it, you have bridged the gaps between yourself, the students, and the task. Use these guiding questions to check whether you are good to go:

- Does the student know what the job is and when it is considered finished? Can she state the purpose in one sentence?

- Does the student know whether or not to bring in her own opinion?

- Does the student know what kind of detail is required?

- Does the student have a vocabulary tool box, consisting of a content area word bank?

- Does the student know who the audience is and what level/style of language to use?

- Does the student know what *not* to do?

- Does the student know what resources she is expected to use?

- Does the student know how to avoid producing an encyclopedia report?

- Does the student know the presentation expectations regarding the appearance and literacy level required?

- Does the student know how to use prior knowledge in addressing the topic?

SUMMARY

Success in a writing task depends upon the thinking that has gone into framing the task so that it is:

♦ **Specific**

The student has clear, well-defined parameters in terms of content and length.

♦ **Structured**

The student approaches the task in a *procedural* fashion, knowing that the process involves preparation, step-by-step engagement, and follow-up.

♦ **Interactive**

The student has the opportunity to make meaning of the new information by fitting it into the context of what she already knows about the subject.

♦ **Serious**

The student sees the importance of the task modeled in its presentation by the teacher. The teacher demonstrates seriousness of purpose by presenting the task with obvious care, planning, and attention to detail.

Framing the task goes hand-in-hand with evaluation. Students are successful when they know what is expected but they still have enough leeway to grow within the task, to experiment a little, to take intellectual risks. As we frame tasks, we should remember that the purpose of writing is to communicate something that is worth saying. Our job is to help students do this, show them how well they've done it, and then help them communicate just a little bit better next time.

3

SUPPORT
MAKING THE CASE

CHAPTER OVERVIEW

This chapter provides various structures, models, and suggestions that answer these questions:

- How can I get students to be specific?
- How can I get students to make fine distinctions of terms in my subject area?
- How can I get students to provide detail?
- How can I get students to justify what they claim?
- Is there anything I can do about the spelling problem?

* * *

SPECIFYING

STRATEGY 1: SHARPENING

EXAMPLE 1

Robbie was asked to explain how aspirin works to relieve pain.

When a person has an ache or pain the body makes substances called prostaglandins. Some prostaglandins cause fever, headaches, and swelling. When you take aspirin, you stop the production of prostaglandins. Aspirin can also cause stomach irritation.

DIAGNOSIS AND PRESCRIPTION

Robbie has a *general* idea of how aspirin works to relieve pain, but he is describing the process too broadly. By referring to prostaglandins as *substances*, he misses the opportunity to use the more specific term *enzyme*. The strength of the support lies in terminology and classification. Broad terminology leads to superficial analysis: Classified terminology leads to careful analysis, as we make finer and finer distinctions along the way.

BIOLOGY

51

COURSE OF TREATMENT

- ◆ Avoid the term *substance*. Say exactly what the substance is.

- ◆ Get to the bottom: Once we sharpen *substance* into *enzyme*, we can specify that the hormone in question is prostaglandin. There are two types of prostaglandins:

  Enzyme: Prostaglandin

  Prostaglandin H_2 synthase (PGH-2): results in pain and fever
  Prostaglandin H_1 synthase (PGH-1): protects the stomach

- ◆ Make distinctions and tell their significance:

REVISION

Aspirin works to relieve pain and fever but it also irritates the stomach. The body produces an enzyme called prostaglandin. There are two kinds of prostaglandin: H_2 synthase (PGH-2), which causes pain and fever, and Pgh-1, which protects the stomach. Aspirin inhibits the function of both of these types of prostaglandin, Scientists don't yet know how to get aspirin to act on PGH-2 while not irritating the stomach by acting on PGH-1.

After writing a sentence or two, Robbie should identify all key terms and determine which ones should be reduced into more specific components. Having the components, Robbie should consider the distinctions between them.

EXAMPLE 2

In the next example, Mitch was asked to explain what a forestry technician does:

A forestry technician cares for trees and takes care of any problems that trees might have. She also does things to prevent forest fires. A forestry technician learns about trees, forests, and conservation. She makes decisions about cutting down trees and planting. To be a forestry technician, you have to have special training.

DIAGNOSIS AND PRESCRIPTION

Mitch has covered a lot of territory but thinks he has no more to say. Actually, each of the sentences here could serve as a topic sentence for a well-developed paragraph.

Paragraph One: Reduce the word *problems* into its components: *blight, unfavorable water conditions, fires, decimation by industry, erosion.*

Paragraph Two: Reduce the words *does things to prevent forest fires: educates campers/hikers and industrialists, monitors rainfall and conditions conducive to fires, monitors activities of users of the forest.*

Paragraph Three: Reduce the words *learns about trees . . . special training: What are the sources of ongoing information about forest life? What formal education is required and where is this training available?*

INTERDIS-CIPLINARY

One of the major causes of Writer's Agony is that the writer feels she doesn't have enough to say on the subject. At the same time, the teacher feels that the writing lacks substance. If we train students to recognize non-specific words in their writing, and teach them to reduce these words into components, they will produce writing which has rich detail, rather than unsupported generalities. The general statement, then, serves as the topic sentence.

SOCIAL STUDIES

- ◆ General: *Spain consists of many different ethnic groups.*
- ◆ Specific: *Although Spain is mostly ethnically homogeneous, some minority groups include the Basques, Galatians, and Catalans.*
- ◆ Analysis: By specifying three ethnic groups, we also find it necessary to clarify the statement even further by stipulating that Spain consists mostly of the majority ethnic group.
- ◆ General: *Jacob Lawrence was influenced by other artists.*
- ◆ Specific: *Jacob Lawrence's mural "Games" is similar to Picasso's "Guernica" in the portrayal of excited crowds and figures that seem to jump out of the frame.*
- ◆ Analysis: Anytime we say "other" we are obliged to stipulate whom we mean. In comparing *Games* to *Guernica*, the writer can't help but notice two key similarities between Picasso and Lawrence.

GENERALITY WORDS

The following words, appropriate for topic sentences, need to be factored into specific components to provide support.

areas	contributions	influence	often	some
bad	decisions	kinds of	positive	steps
causes	differences	major	problems	things
challenges	good	many	reasons	types of
changes	important	negative	several	various

TEACHING THROUGH VISUALS

Teach students to make branch diagrams that display relationships between generalities and specifics.

GENERALITIES AND SPECIFICS

To train students to stretch their thinking and language, have them construct a continuum that shows how words grow from specific examples to general concepts. For example,

Hudson/Rivers/bodies of water/geographical features

STRATEGY 2: PROVIDE DETAIL

By *detail*, we mean specifics of time and place, who and what. An essay that is liberally supplied with prepositional phrases—time and place words—will provide detail. Whether you teach English or any other subject, prepositional phrases are easy to teach. If you hesitate to use grammatical terminology, just say "time and place words."

PREPOSITIONS: WORDS THAT GIVE TIME AND PLACE

about	before	concerning	off	under
above	behind	down	on	underneath
across	below	during	over	until
after	beneath	except	past	unto
against	beside	for	since	up
along	besides	from	through	upon
amid	between	in	throughout	with
among	beyond	into	to	within
around	but (except)	like	toward	without
at	by	of		

Consider the following writing task:

> Between the years 1865 and 1914, industrialization deeply changed the working and private lives of the working class in the United States. Identify three areas of life for the working class which were affected by industrialization and show how individuals, organizations, and the government responded to these changes.

This is how the writer can use our list of prepositional phrases to provide detail and support:

- *during* the post Civil War years . . .
- *across* the South
- *in* 1898
- *for* safer working conditions
- *below* the poverty line
- *after* the Pullman strike
- *between* labor and management
- *by* Russell Cornwell *in Acres of Diamonds*, written *in* 1900
- *by* Samuel Gompers
- *at* Carnegie Steel Company *in* 1892
- *before* the Haymarket affair

TEACHING THROUGH VISUALS

Whether you teach English or any other subject, post a list of prepositions in your classroom or on your Website to remind students to add detail.

SOCIAL STUDIES

STRATEGY 3: FACTS AND FIGURES

Dates, time spans, numbers of people, proportions, distances, expenses, statistics: Every issue entails numbers. When we support our assertions, descriptions, explanations with numbers, we're establishing credibility. Consider the following DBQs (document-based-questions) in terms of how numbers play a part:

> How and why did the lives and status of Northern middle-class women change between 1776 and 1876?

Numbers

- ◆ Demographics: How did the population change because of war and immigration?

- ◆ Economics: Discuss issues of wages and expenses. Discuss the economic issues of household management.

- ◆ Dates and time spans: What pivotal events took place at what dates? What time spans represented watershed or subtle changes?

> Analyze the changes that occurred during the 1960s in the goals, strategies, and support of the movement for African American civil rights.

Numbers

- ◆ Demographics: How many people participated in key civil rights demonstrations? What percentage of blacks lived in poverty as compared to whites? What were the statistical differences in education? How did the Civil Rights Act affect these statistics by the close of the decade?

- ◆ Economics: What was the disparity in income between blacks and whites in America during the 1960s?

- ◆ Dates and time spans: When did the march on Washington take place? What is the significance of the following years: 1964? 1968?

TEACH THROUGH VISUALS

Aside from statistics, dates, time spans and amounts, students should remember ordinals and comparatives. Post the following words in your classroom or on your Website:

first	fewer, fewest	minimum
second	less, least	maximum
last	more, most	

This simple list will remind students to include information about quantities and to show the relative meaning of specific numbers.

STRATEGY 4: NAMES AND PLACES

Like numbers, names and places are specific details. Any writing in the humanities should have a cast of characters and a setting. The Document-Based-Question requires background information to supplement information that is directly found in the document. To include names and places, the writer can address these questions:

Names (in a humanities issue)

♦ Who is/are the leader(s) of the issue in question?

♦ Who is/are the opponent(s) of the leader(s)?

♦ What group is associated with this issue?

♦ Who influenced or was influenced by the leader?

♦ What is the time period? What is this time period known as?

Names (in a science or technology issue)

♦ Is there a specific person or institution associated with this topic?

♦ Does the topic have a history of theories posited by various people?

♦ Can you start off with an interesting quote?

♦ Can you include an anecdote that "humanizes" the concept?

Places (in a humanities issue)

♦ Is this issue associated with a particular place?

♦ How do geographical features play a role in this issue?

♦ If this issue involves transportation and communication, how has it branched out from the original place?

Places (in a science issue)

♦ Is this issue associated with a particular place?

♦ Is there a particular population subgroup that would be especially affected by this issue?

♦ Are there ecological or geographical features about a particular place that effect this issue?

JUSTIFYING

An essay is about justifying a thesis; it is about supporting a main idea. We make a claim and then we have to prove that it's true. The term thesis statement is one of those academic terms, like theme (to which is related), that is variously defined. Some teachers assert that a thesis statement must be arguable; others think of a thesis statement as the main topic sentences. In terms of development, there are four types of expository essays:

1. A *position paper* asserts an arguable claim and then justifies it with reasons, theories and examples:

   The treatment of circus animals constitutes animal cruelty.

   In a position paper, the writer needs to refute the opposition by acknowledging the arguments on the other side, and then responding to these arguments. The refutation can come at either the beginning or the end of the paper and should not overwhelm the writer's own main arguments. The purpose of the position paper is to persuade.

2. An *interpretative/descriptive paper* explicates a text and/or reveals the writer's knowledge of a particular topic by presenting reasons and examples.

   Nationalism and imperialism have caused military aggression at least three times in the twentieth century.

   The purpose of the interpretative/descriptive paper is to inform.

3. A *cause/effect paper* lays out causative factors and shows how they are directly or indirectly related to the result:

   In the 1930s, four factors contributed to the migration to California of people who lived in the Dust Bowl States.

   The purpose of the cause/effect paper is to show a relationship.

4. A *statistical paper* demonstrates understanding of the meaning of numbers to the topic:

   Teenage smoking has increased in the past five years.

   This writer will then be expected to do more than present statistics, which could just as easily be expressed on a graph or chart. The writer of the statistical paper must explain why numbers are falling into a particular trend, what factors operate on the issue, what are the implications of the figures in terms of past and future.

REGARDING SPELLING

As a general rule, spelling becomes more challenging the deeper we go into a subject. There are several reasons for this:

♦ The more specific words of a subject area are the ones less frequently used in speech or seen in writing. Example: *chemical, enzyme, amylase.*

♦ Technical terms are likely to be of Greek origin. Words of Greek origin tend to have eccentric spellings: *phylum, pheromone, oligarchy, chromatic.*

♦ Technical terms tend to be long because they consist of prefixes, suffixes, and roots.

- We usually can't spell words that we can't pronounce. Technical words are likely to be unfamiliar to the novice's ear and mouth, as well as to her pen.

- Technical terms may not be in the computer's spellchecker.

Justin avoids using words he can't spell. The result is a juvenile style. Justin doesn't use much technical vocabulary, and his content is superficial. It makes all the difference in the world if Justin has a pre-writing spelling list, especially when he has to copy out the words once or twice. He uses such a list not only for spelling, but also to help him think of ideas.

DETAILS

PRE-WRITING SPELLING LIST

Topic: The ancient Egyptians developed many important technologies which were the building blocks of later societies. Discuss three achievements of the ancient Egyptians and show how these achievements were built upon by later societies.

Egyptians	*Egyptians*
civilization	*civilization*
hieroglyphics	*hieroglyphics*
knowledge	*knowledge*
mathematical	*mathematical*
architecture/architectural	*architecture/architectural*
priests	*priests*
calendar	*calendar*
surgery	*surgery*
symbols	*symbols*
medical	*medical*
achievements	*achievements*
Pharaoh	*Pharaoh*
burial	*burial*

SUMMARY: SUPPORT AND SPECIFICITY

EIGHT CLASSROOM PRACTICES

- Ask each sentence to give you more information: *Which one? Why? Where?*

  A well-developed paragraph should answer several questions about the words in the topic sentence.

- Sharpen key terms:

  Beware of IT: Subject all ITs to ruthless scrutiny. The word IT is often non-specific and vaguely referenced. Ask every IT what IT is. More than two ITs in a paragraph exceed federal guidelines.

SOCIAL STUDIES

Reduce key terms into their components. Create a continuum line which shows the gradations of a particular noun: What words are more general? more specific?

♦ Use "time and place" words:

Provide detail

♦ Include the numbers:

Consider how statistics, proportions, dates, and time spans affect the issue.

Make it a practice to include numbers in every paragraph.

♦ Include names and places (proper nouns):

Make it a practice to have *capital letter words* in every paragraph.

♦ Cross out unnecessary words:

Get rid of redundancies that clutter up the sentence and impede meaning.

♦ Use technical terminology:

Talk the talk: Resist the temptation to dumb down your speech. Use technical terms and define them in context

List tech terms: Give students every chance to see and hear key terms before and after the lesson.

♦ Spelling:

Lists: As a whole class or in cooperative learning groups, generate topic-specific spelling lists. Have students keep spelling journals. For continuous visual reinforcement, display a cumulative spelling list in the classroom.

Learn words in groups: Technical terms often fall into etymological categories. Words are easier to remember when grouped with similar words. Words which are spelled similarly usually have similar meaning: *oligarchy, monarchy, hierarchy.*

Topic: Vascular plants have stems, which come in two types. Discuss the two types of stems, give examples, and tell the functions of the parts of the stems.

Stems

There are two main categories of plants: nonvascular and vascular. Nonvascular plants have no stems. Algae, liverwort, and moss are nonvascular plants.

Vascular plants have stems. There are two types of stems: woody (ferns, flowering plants, trees, shrubs) and herbaceous (annuals).

Woody stems have five parts. The cork is the outer layer and it consists of dead cells. The cork is hard in order to protect the stem from diseases and predators. The next layer is the cortex which consists of living cells. The cortex stores food. The food is transported to the leaves and roots by the phloem. The cambium causes stems to thicken as the plant ages and its function is to separate the phloem from the xylem. The xylem consists of living, tube-like cells which act like the plumbing system, delivering water throughout the plant. The xylem provides firm support so that the plant can survive season after season.

Herbaceous plants don't usually survive from season to seasons. Because they have less xylem, they have soft stems. The outer layer is the spongy cortex, and the xylem and phloem within the cortex are arranged in patterns, rather than in concentric circles as with the woody stem.

The content here is unadorned, but it gets the job done in clear, concise, appropriate language. The sentences are stripped clean of distractive elements and the writer demonstrates confidence and control of spatial and functional relationships.

DO I HAVE ENOUGH SUPPORT
A SELF-CHECK FOR STUDENTS

Consider three paragraphs in your draft in terms of the following:

Specific key terms			
Prepositional Phrases ("time and place" words)			
Numbers			
Names			
Places			
Each paragraph answers questions			
Use of technical language			
Words correctly spelled			
Each paragraph has a topic sentence			
No unnecessary words			

4

SHORT STATEMENTS
IN FIFTY WORDS OR LESS . . .

CHAPTER OVERVIEW

We don't always want students to write full essays. This chapter presents models for writing statements of one or two well-developed sentences (fifty words or so) that have high information density. The models in this chapter answer these questions:

♦ How can I get students to write *brief identifications* of people, places, and events?

♦ How can I get students to write statements that *show contrast?*

♦ How can I get students to show that they understand *cause/effect, assumptions, and tenets of my subject area?*

The idea is to show writers how they can concentrate as many facts as possible into a small space. By doing so, the writer is efficient, concise, and direct.

These statements are useful for topic sentences and also as responses on in-class tests, where students need to deliver information in concentrated format.

THE BRIEF BIO

We ask for a brief identification statement for a historical figure. Without instruction, Michele might say something like this:

Benito Mussolini was known as Il Duce. He was one of the most extraordinary men of the Twentieth Century. Benito Mussolini was born on July 29, 1883. He was the head of the Fascist party in Italy. During the mid 1930's, Mussolini engaged in a highly aggressive foreign policy. He formed an alliance with Adolf Hitler.

Michele did some homework and knows facts, but her style here is inefficient and the order in which she presents the information conveys that she does not understand the most notable aspects of Mussolini's place in history.

SOCIAL STUDIES

61

THE TASK OF THE BRIEF BIO

◆ Tell the action of the person that makes him or her notable in history.

◆ Place the person in a historical context of time and place. Usually, this will involve mention of a major historical event or period, as well as a span of years.

◆ Give any sound bytes or key phrases, such as nicknames, associated with the person.

◆ Present a positive or negative view of the person, if applicable.

◆ Use compact, concise language. Make every word count.

WHAT *NOT* TO DO IN THE BRIEF BIO

◆ Do not tell about the person's childhood. Information about a person's childhood is usually not wanted in a secondary school report unless the teacher specifically asks for it. Usually, such information merely serves to get the paper off to a slow and painful start.

◆ Do not use empty words such as *extraordinary, remarkable, important*. The fact that this person is a historical figure assumes that these words apply to them in some way, but words of this nature tell nothing specific about the person.

MODEL BRIEF BIOS

Benito Mussolini, known as Il Duce, led the Italian Fascist Party in the 1930's and 40's, during World War II. He is known for brutal aggressiveness against Ethiopia and Albania and for turning Italy into a police state.

Sigmund Freud, an Austrian physician, opened up the world of the subconscious mind. In the late 19th/early 20th Centuries, Freud developed a theory of psychoanalysis which was based on the influence of memories upon behavior and personality.

Rene Descartes (1596-1650) refined the scientific method and invented analytic geometry. His form of reasoning, founded on mathematical principles, is known as the method of rational deduction.

Stephen W. Hawking is a contemporary physicist whose book <u>A Brief History of Time</u> presents a theory about the age and development of the universe.

In the above examples, the writer has to cut away all secondary information in the interest of conciseness. To do this, we rely on strong action words:

ACTION WORDS OF THE BRIEF BIO

Following is a list of action words that will do yeoman's service in the brief bio. By using these action words, the student can't help but name the chief accomplishment of the person.

INTERDIS-
CIPLINARY

annexed	destroyed	gave	led	refined
attacked	developed	headed	obtained	ruined
based	discovered	influenced	opened	started
built	establish	instituted	opposed	studied
challenged	explained	invaded	presented	theorized that
conquered	exposed	invented	questioned	won
created	fought for	killed	rebelled against	wrote
defended	founded			

As we all know to our chagrin, students like to copy directly out of reference books. By requiring (and teaching the form of) the brief bio, we encourage students to write in their own words, to *paraphrase*.

START WITH KEY WORDS/PHRASES

The student writes three key words that describe the subject's accomplishments.

Henry Ford:	*automobile production*	*affordable*	*antiunionist*
John Meynard Keynes:	*economics*	*government policies*	*Great Depression*

CONNECTORS

After establishing the key words, we need connectors. Without connectors, we'd have a string of uninteresting sentences, each bearing only one unit of meaning.

based on	for whom	which helped to	which led to
derived from	is known as	which is	whose
for which	is known for		

Henry Ford <u>is known for</u> establishing assembly line production which made the Model T affordable to middle class Americans.

John Meynard Keynes developed an economic theory <u>based on</u> governmental policies which controlled demand by

CONNOTATION

There's nothing wrong with a student's having an opinion about a person in history, or science, or the arts. In fact, we do want students to have an emotional investment in their subjects. What we don't want is the "empty word" sentence referred to above. That is, an entire sentence is spent on informing the reader that the subject was "extraordinary." Instead, we want the student's opinion to be expressed in terms of word choice, *connotation*. *Connotation* can be explained to students as the *emotional freight* of a word. Most of the action words in the list above bear emotional freight. We can have students convey their feelings about how their subjects changed the world for good or ill by using connotative action words: Did Columbus *discover* America or did he *invade* it? Did Mussolini *lead* the Italians or did he *oppress* them?

When learning how to use connotation, two convenient sources are the textbook and the newspaper. What words can be substituted with words of similar literal meaning but different connotations? How do the good guys become the bad guys?

> *Eamon De Valera declared Ireland independent of Britain in 1937.*

We ascribe a Jeffersonian heroism with the words *declared . . . independent*, as opposed to:

> *Under the leadership of Eamon De Valera, Ireland broke away from Britain in 1937.*

or

> *In 1937 Ireland was established as a separate republic by Eamon De Valera.*

An awareness of connotation is one of the most important language skills a reader or writer can have. Connotation delivers the subtext, the attitude, that shapes our response to the message.

PLACES/EVENTS

The brief bio and the places/events statement are useful for the document-based question (DBQ) because the writer is asked to demonstrate knowledge of the historical context of the document. As he must do this without lapsing into wordy summary, the type of writing which we are demonstrating in this chapter is worth practicing. This type of writing, condensed as it is, establishes the basics and frees the writer to discuss the issue on a more elevated level.

We ask for a brief identification of an event. Without instruction, the student might say something like this:

> *The Crimean War was fought between 1853 and 1856. It was fought between Russia and Britain, France, Turkey and Sardinia. Russia had wanted to expand out to Mediterranean ports. The Allied forces were trying to protect Turkish provinces. The major battles were Sevastopol and Balaklava. The Allied forces won.*

Given an expense account of fifty words, this writer could get more for her money by using the language more efficiently:

> *The Crimean War (1853-1856) was a territorial clash. Russia sought expansion and aggressed into Mediterranean ports which were Turkish provinces, and Turkey, whose allies were Britain, France, and Sardinia. The*

Allied forces won, after victories at Sevastopol and Balaklava. Florence Nightingale pioneered modern nursing methods during the Crimean War.

THE TASK OF THE PLACE/EVENT STATEMENT

♦ Tell the date(s).

♦ Tell the major players (individuals or countries)

♦ Give at least one detail that will make the event memorable.

♦ Tell the outcome of the event.

♦ Use compact, concise language. Make every word count.

WHAT *NOT* TO DO IN THE PLACE/EVENT STATEMENT

♦ Don't take up a whole sentence to give the date. Put the date in parentheses after the first mention of the event, as above.

♦ As with the brief, don't waste words by using empty words.

♦ Don't write a string of short sentences. Instead, combine sentences so that the reader sees connections and relationships

MODEL PLACE/EVENT STATEMENTS

The Battle of the Coral Sea (May 4-8, 1942) was a naval battle between US and Japan. It was the first naval battle fought entirely by aircraft launched from carriers. Although the US suffered more casualties, Japan was impeded from advancing toward New Guinea.

The Sacco-Vanzetti Case (1921) was a murder trial in Braintree, Mass., which turned into a showdown between conservatives and liberals. Although the two immigrants were convicted of murdering a paymaster, liberals contend that they were railroaded by conservatives. Sacco and Vanzetti, Italian-born anarchists and draft-evaders, were executed in 1927.

The Pullman Strike (May-July 1894) and boycott of rolling stock was led by Eugene V. Debs' American Railway Union. The union protested the Pullman Company's wage cuts and retaliations against unionists. The labor movement suffered a great blow when the strike was crushed by federal troops.

The Reformation (16th Century) was a time of religious and political unrest, leading to the establishment of Protestantism. Reformers such as Martin Luther and John Wycliffe denied papal authority and led movements away from the R.C. Church. Protestantism spread throughout Germany, England, and the low Countries.

By living within the budget of fifty words, the writer is forced to discern the primary from the secondary, and must construct high-density sentences, which, as in the brief bio, depend on strong action words.

SOCIAL STUDIES

ACTION WORDS OF EVENTS

acted against	changed	grew	opposed	revolutionized
activated	contended	influenced	overcame	spread
attacked	developed into	invented	prevented	stopped
brought	fought	led to	protested	turned into

Events are about *change* and/or *conflict*. Those that are primarily about change (the Industrial Revolution, immigration, natural disasters) have an element of conflict because conflict always results from change. Those that are about conflict (war, protest) are also about change because conflict always are the result of or the cause of change. In writing the place/event statement, we should consider how conflict and change are related: What change results from or causes the conflict? What conflict results from the change?

CONNECTORS

is associated with	such as	was the first	was a time of
is known for	was a conflict between	was the last	was typical of
marked a turning point	was established	was led by	which led to

QUESTIONS ABOUT EVENTS

* Is the event finite or did it fade in and out in time?
* How is this event like other events in its own time and in other historical contexts?
* How is this event a result of its antecedents? How is it a cause of events that came later?
* Is this a natural event or a man-made event? If a natural event, how did man-made responses play a role? If a man-made event, how did nature play a role?
* In terms of human involvement, who was the leader? Who were the opponents? Were groups, organized or unorganized, involved? Are slogans associated with this event?
* How is this event notable? Is it the first (or last) of its kind? Is it notable because of its success or because of its failure?
* Does this event represent the nobility of man or does it represent cruelty? In what ways does it represent both positive and negative human characteristics.?
* How does science/technology play a role in this event?
* What visual images are associated with this event?

NOTES: The McCarthy Era

Time Frame	1948-mid 50s	
Similar events	Salem witch trials/Dreyfus Affair	
Before/After	Before: WWII; estab. of Iron Curtain in Europe; division of Germany During/After: Cold War	
Notability	Notable because of damage to reputations; naming names; betrayals	
Natural/Man-made	Man-made	
Leadership	Wis. Sen. Joseph McCarthy HUAC Richard Nixon	Lawrence Welch Pres. Truman Arthur Miller
Success/Failure	Failed to deliver justice; damaged credibility of House; led to ruined careers	
Human Nature: Noble/Ignoble	Ignoble; power hunger; irresponsible accusations	
Science/Technology	Early days of TV; public exposure	
Visual Image	Senate hearings: Lawrence Welch (Have you no shame) Wheeling, W. Va. (I have here in my hand . . .)	

THE CONTRAST STATEMENT

Another form of the high-density information statement is the contrast statement, in which the writer expresses a paradox, ironic contrast, or the co-existence of two extremes. Simply put, a contrast statement is a statement which contains a pair of opposites. The intellectual power of the contrast statement is that, as the writer balances contradictions, she establishes the dynamic tension that operates between opposites.

THE TASK OF THE CONTRAST STATEMENT

♦ Present the opposing terms and show the relationship between them.

♦ Clarify the direction in which things are moving, if applicable.

♦ Present the information in an orderly manner so that we know what refers to what.

◆ Use parallel structure (similar grammatical format). The contrast statement should have an even, predictable flow.

◆ Use compact, precise language.

WHAT *NOT* TO DO IN THE CONTRAST STATEMENT

◆ Don't overuse pronouns such as *it, this, that, which*. Be careful to clarify the nouns to which these pronouns refer.

◆ Don't simply present opposites: Show how the two opposing forces turn into one another or how they act in conflict to cause change or maintain equilibrium.

◆ Avoid *not*. Instead of negating a concept with *not*, use the proper terminology.

MODEL CONTRAST STATEMENTS

The appearance of the moon depends upon the amount of its surface that is lit up by the sun. We see a "full moon" when the moon nears the side of the Earth opposite the sun. We see no image of the moon when it passes between the Earth and the sun.

One example of action/reaction is a jet spray. Jet sprays are produced when a force acts in the opposite direction of the flow.

Decomposers act to break down dead organisms, turning them into nutrients which support other life forms.

Warm and moist climates produce the greatest amount of chemical weathering, while cold and dry climates produce the least amount of chemical weathering.

WHY THINK ABOUT CONTRASTS

Like the organizational strategy of sorting and classifying, thinking in terms of contrast is one way to make order out of chaos. Consider how much of our academic information is about the interplay of opposite forces: mathematics, physics, chemistry, art, music, poetry. And we can think of any historical or social issue as the struggle between opponents. Thinking in contrasts helps us to organize and remember information.

SETTING UP THE CONTRAST STATEMENT

In one model, a contrast statement consists of two opposing forces, an action word that expresses the relationship between them, and a conjunction (or joining word) that connects the two forces. A semicolon can also serve as a connector.

EARTH
SCIENCE

ACTION WORDS OF CONTRAST

antagonize	compete	force	push
attack	complement	increase	rebel
balance	counter	match	repel
battle	decrease	offset	reverse
break down	equalize	oppose	slow down
combat	erode	protest	speed up
compensate	fight	pull	wear down

TYPES OF CONTRAST

THE SIMPLE COMPARISON

The simple comparison shows the relationship from one extreme to another. Consider the interplay of opposites in these sentences about the basic tenets of earth science.

- ◆ Establishment of opposite viewpoints: A supports this, but B supports that.

  Laissez-faire policies allow business to operate freely, but strong government intervention policies control business practices.

  - Application: Write several sentences which establish two opposite views on a given subject.
  - Connection: *, but*

- ◆ Directionality: A moves from Point B to Point C.

  Winds blow from regions of high pressure to regions of low pressure.

  - Application: Write several sentences based on this pattern: Show how something moves in opposite directions.
  - Connection: *from/to*

- ◆ Two sides of a continuum: A and B represent the extremes of C.

  The hardest mineral is diamond, which can scratch any other mineral. The softest is talc, which cannot scratch any other mineral.

  - Application: Write several sentences which explain the characteristics of the most and the least of a particular concept.
  - Connection: *est . . . est*

- ◆ Reasoning: C determines the contrast in reactions between A and B.

  Because land has a lower specific heat than water, land heats up faster than water.

  - Application: Write several sentences which show why Condition A causes different responses in Condition B and Condition C.
  - Connection: Because . . . , _____(. . . er)___than . . .

CONCURRENCE

A more sophisticated level of the contrast statement presents two opposing elements which occur simultaneously. A acts against B because both are happening at the same time.

- ◆ Challenge: A disrupts the status quo (B).

  The migration patterns caused by industrialization in Latin America have posed a challenge to elite, land-owning families. As the urban middle class aligns with the laboring poor, the upper class loses power.

  - Application: Write several sentences which show how one force introduces changes which disrupt the status quo.
  - Connection: *. . . pose a challenge to. As . . .*

- ◆ Erosion: A erodes B.

  Pebbles lose their sharp edges, becoming rounded, as they travel downstream. As they travel, their sharp edges are worn away by objects which they strike.

  - Application: Write several sentences which show how one force diminishes another by acting upon it over time.
  - Connection: *as . . .*

- ◆ Balance: A keeps B in check.

  In a first-class lever, the fulcrum is placed between the effort and the load.

  - Application: Write several sentences in which two opposing forces are kept stable by a balancing point.
  - Connection: *between*

IRONY AND PARADOX: EVEN THOUGH . . .

In transcending the literal, irony and paradox exist on a high intellectual plane. To use an even though statement is to acknowledge a contradiction, a paradox, which is true despite the contrast.

- ◆ Competing forces: A survives the assault of B.

  Even though the Norman rulers in England tried to impose the French language, the English language survived and flourished.

  - Application: Write several sentences which show how a condition exists in the presence of an opposing force which usually undermines this condition.
  - Connection: *even though*

- ◆ Paradox: A appears to deny B, but the statement is true.

  Even people who couldn't read valued books in the Middle Ages.

  - Application: Write several sentences which express a truth which seems to defy logic.
  - Connection: *even*

♦ Cycling: A circles into B:

Endocrine levels are regulated as the level of TSH stimulates the secretion of thyroxin, which, in turn, triggers the reduction of TSH as proper thyroxin levels are reached.

- Application: Write several sentences which express how equilibrium is reached by a cycle of increasing and decreasing levels.

- Connection: *which, in turn,*

USING THE SEMICOLON TO EXPRESS CONTRAST

Using a semicolon is an efficient way to present a contrast statement. A semicolon is used to separate two statements, each of which could stand alone as a complete sentence. The semicolon implies equality between the statements on either side of it. A semicolon works best when both statements follow the same grammatical pattern:

Insolation hits the surface almost vertically near the Equator; insolation hits at a more glancing angle near the Poles.

The air temperature is usually higher than the water temperature near the Equator; the air temperature is usually lower than the water temperature near the Poles.

Humans are placental animals; marsupials are nonplacental.

A semicolon can be used to create symmetry. This symmetry works as a memory aid, as it organizes information along a parallel course. If we think of learning as making order out of chaos, then we can see the value of using semicolons to arrange information and to show similar relationships.

GIVING EXAMPLES

A well-developed piece should be replete with examples. The trouble is, like the words *in conclusion*, the words *for example* wear on one's nerves after the first few thousand times. Not only that, but here's what often happens when novice writers give examples:

The pituitary gland secretes numerous hormones. For example, a growth-stimulating hormone, a thyroid-stimulating hormone, and a follicle-stimulating hormone.

It commonly happens that, as above, the sentence that opens with *for example* is not a sentence but a fragment. We can eliminate this error by replacing for example with a colon:

The pituitary gland secretes numerous hormones: a growth-stimulating hormone, a thyroid-stimulating hormone and a follicle-stimulating hormone.

EARTH SCIENCE

BIOLOGY

BIOLOGY

Many people associate a colon with the words *as follows*. Although *as follows* can be used with a colon, since a colon already means as follows, the words *as follows* are actually redundant. Concise writing requires you to just make the statement, end with a colon, and then present the list of examples. The words *such as* (or even *for example,* if not overused) can be used instead of a colon to introduce an example or a list.

THE CAUSE/EFFECT STATEMENT

The cause/effect statement usually bears content area terminology, and this density of information challenges the reader/writer to handle both the relationship and the terms. Thus, the construction of the cause/effect statement should be as simple as possible so that rereadings aren't necessary. Without instruction, the writer might construct a cause/effect statement like this:

> *Radioactive decay is when energy is given off by unstable isotopes that disintegrate. Subatomic particles can also be given off.*

The problem here is disorganization and indirectness. The indirectness is caused by passive voice, a wordy grammatical construction which usually tacks on a *by . . .* phrase.

In the revision below, the writer has presented the cause/effect relationship in an orderly, sequential manner:

> *In the process of radioactive decay, unstable isotopes disintegrate. As they do, they emit energy and/or subatomic particles.*

THE TASK OF THE CAUSE/EFFECT STATEMENT

♦ Clarify the sequence and the relationship: what causes what?

♦ Clarify whether the causative agent can bring about the result by itself, or if the causative agent is one of many causes.

♦ Write short sentences if long sentences would confuse the meaning.

WHAT *NOT* TO DO IN THE CAUSE/EFFECT STATEMENT

♦ Don't overuse prepositional phrases, especially those containing technical terms.

♦ Don't allow the sentence to double back on itself. Keep the sequence in order.

♦ Don't jam too many technical terms into too small a space. Spread out the words so that the reader can clearly see relationships.

How can we recognize the cause/effect structure? We're in cause/effect territory when we can illustrate that something happened as a result of some force or the interaction of multiple forces. A cause/effect statement answers the question *How do we get . . .?*

> *When genetic information is transferred from one organism to another, the result is recombinant DNA. Recombinant DNA introduces new genes into an organism so that the cell can reproduce according to the newly introduced information.*

> *The fall of Communism in 1991 led to internecine warfare in Eastern Europe. After Croatia was recognized as an independent state, fierce fighting broke out among nationalistic groups in the former Yugoslavia.*

> *The signing of the Camp David Accords by Egypt and Israel in 1979 led to Israeli retreat from Egyptian territories. As a result, Egypt recognized Israeli sovereignty.*

MODELS

ACTION WORDS OF CAUSE/EFFECT

as a result of	effect (as action word)	induce	produce
bring about	generate	influence	result in
cause	give rise to	lead to	trigger
create	grow		

In the fifty word statement, the first sentence establishes the cause/effect relationship. The second sentence follows through by refining the effect, showing what happens next.

We lead students to make the cause/effect statement by asking them to track changes:

♦ What is the change?

♦ What caused the change?

♦ What will happen next?

SEQUENCE WORDS

after	next	then
first	so that	when

Social studies essays often require the cause/effect structure. Typically, students are asked to connect a particular event to the change which it wrought. Because one change leads to another, we can consider acute (immediate) changes to be those which accrue to long-term changes. The long-term changes are more sweeping than the acute changes, as shown below:

BIOLOGY

SOCIAL STUDIES

SOCIAL STUDIES

Events (Causes)	Acute Changes (Effects)	Long Term Changes (Effects of Effects)
Voyages of Columbus	Began European settlement of Americas Decimated indigenous populations	Extensive cultural diffusion, especially Latin America
Glorious Revolution	Parliament established Limitation of power of monarchy	Indirect form of democracy
Failure of Weimar Republic	Lack of confidence in government Severe economic troubles	Ascendancy of Nazi dictatorship

From Osborne, John, Sue Ann Kime, and Regina O'Donnell. 1988, 1993. *N & N Global Studies Review Text.* Middletown, NY: N & N, p. 447.

ASSUMPTIONS AND TENETS

In academic study, we make assumptions and hold tenets. These tenets are only as useful as our ability to apply them and to understand their implications. The fifty-word statement can encapsulate both the tenet and the application:

THE TASK OF THE ASSUMPTION/TENET STATEMENT

♦ Make a clear, concise statement of the assumption/tenet.

♦ In the next sentence, show how the assumption/tenet can be extended, specified, or applied. Or, explain the implications of this tenet: what does it lead us to think of?

♦ If the assumption/tenet is dense with technical information, write an *in other words* statement.

MODELS

BIOLOGY

The Hardy-Weinberg Principle: The gene pool of a population tends to remain about the same if four conditions exist:
♦ large populations with equal gender numbers
♦ random mating
♦ minimal mixing in of other populations
♦ minimal chromosomal mutation

Application: This principle can rarely be applied in current worldwide conditions because of extensive migration, resulting in mixing of populations.

Mendel's Principle: Characteristics are inherited as a result of the transmission of hereditary factors.

Implication: Hereditary factors can be controlled by isolating and manipulating genes.

Game theory: In a game with two players, each player must take into account the possible strategies of the other. In a zero-sum game, if one side's loss is inversely proportionate to the other's gain.

Refinement: Von Neumann's "minimax theorem" states that by using a combination of mixed strategies, playing the probabilities, and making random moves, each player can reach his optimal result.

The second law of thermodynamics: Any change in an isolated system increases entropy.

Clarification: Entropy is the degree of disorder in a physical system. The above law Implication: Any change in an isolated system will result in a some degree of disorder.

To extend a principle, we ask these questions:

♦ Is this principle operational? That is, do the condition on which it depends exist in the current world? Have they ever existed to make the principle operational?

♦ What is the significance of this principle? Why know it?

♦ What other assumptions does this principle lead to?

♦ What details do we need to understand regarding this principle?

ACTION WORDS OF ASSUMPTIONS/TENETS

assert	contend	maintain	put forth
assume	hold	posit	state
claim	hypothesize	prove	theorize

LEAD-INS

according to	can be said to	is extended to	therefore
applies to	hence	results in	thus

MATH

PHYSICS

SUMMARY

Teachers are wise to teach the short statement because it is a rigorous exercise in manipulating and expressing information. It is a writing form of precision and conciseness. One of the problems that content area teachers tend to have with writing is that the labor intensiveness of grading a written piece. The short statement eases this problem while at the same time demanding academic rigor.

- Within the framework of the fifty-word statement, express as much information as possible.

- The process for accomplishing this writing task is to make the writing more efficient. We do this by combing through unnecessary words, using colons and semicolons, and using the technical language of the subject.

- The *short statement* usually has two sentences, the second of which is a refinement of the first.

- The *short statement* can be used to introduce a longer writing task or to summarize a topic.

- There are various types of *short statements*, each with their own patterns and key words.

5

VOCABULARY
WORD FOR WORD

CHAPTER OVERVIEW

Central to learning a subject is learning its terminology. All teachers traffic in words, in making students comfortable with the language of the subject. This chapter addresses the following questions:

♦ How can I help students write clear definitions?

♦ How can I help students use new words?

♦ What are the key action words of my subject area?

♦ How can I explain the differences between how words are used in the vernacular and how these words can be used in my subject area?

* * *

Katie has plenty of vocabulary lists: with all the workbook exercises she's done, with all the glossaries she's had her nose in, with all the column A's and column B's she's matched, with all the terms she's used in a sentence, you'd think she'd have more words than a congressional hearing. But the vast majority of these words will never infiltrate their way into Katie's vocabulary, either academically or socially.

Words are to learning what ingredients are to cooking, but it takes more than cursory exposure to know a word. Knowing a word means understanding how it is used in context, its tone, its nuances, its flexibility.

WRITING DEFINITIONS: A WHOLE BRAIN APPROACH

In all content areas, students need to write definitions. Jamie used to write definitions like these:

♦ *Irony is when you get an unexpected thing that happens.*

♦ *Photosynthesis is when plants make food out of sunlight.*

♦ *A geosyncline is sediment that forms a depression in the ground.*

- ◆ *Feudalism is when the serfs work for the landowner.*
- ◆ *The prime rate is what the best customers get charged at the bank.*
- ◆ *Infrastructure is bridges, tunnels, roads and public buildings.*
- ◆ *Detoxify is getting rid of poisons in the body by the liver.*

The angels weep at Jamie's definitions not because she misunderstands the concepts. She obviously has some grasp of what the terms mean, but her language lacks control and professionalism. Her writing is marred by imprecision and lack of grace.

In this section, we present a teaching model for writing definitions using left and right brain thinking. This model involves two types of sentences. The *methodical sentence* is left-brain thinking: it lays out a carefully constructed procedure to explain what a word means. The second sentence, created through right-brain thinking, is the *metaphorical sentence:* it presents the concept using figurative language. By engaging both left and right brain, the student develops a full and lasting understanding of the term.

SENTENCE ONE: LEFT-BRAIN (METHODICAL) THINKING

Jamie's definitions fall apart at the *is when* point. Nothing good ever happened after *is when. Is when* writers do not know how to write a definition. To *define* is to *make finite:* to *delimit,* set boundaries upon a concept, encasing what's inside. Writing a definition, then, is a surgical process, a methodical way of establishing the limits of a concept. To write a good definition, we need to follow these steps:

STEP 1—NOUN

Express the concept as a *noun*. This must be done because a definition tells what *something* is:

- ◆ Irony
- ◆ Photosynthesis
- ◆ A geosyncline
- ◆ Feudalism
- ◆ The prime rate
- ◆ Infrastructure
- ◆ Detoxification

STEP 2—VERB

Follow the *noun or noun phrase* by the verb *is* or *are*.

STEP 3—REALM

Follow the *verb* by *the* or *a*, plus another *noun* that expresses the general category. I'll refer to the general category as the *realm*.

- Irony is *a concurrence . . .*
- Photosynthesis is *a process . . .*
- A geosyncline is *a formation*
- Feudalism is *a system . . .*
- The prime rate is *the rate . . .*
- Infrastructure is *the system . . .*
- Detoxification is *the process . . .*

Other general categories:

approach	event	part	result	tendency
belief	form	pattern	series	theory
condition	interaction	period	situation	trend
consequence	meeting	phase	state	type
development	mixture	philosophy	style	unit
era	occurrence	relationship	structure	way of life

A *realm* is a general area, a field. Each subject area has a general list of categories which are most applicable. Sometimes, we have to work backwards. It took a while for us to come up with *concurrence*. We played around with *situation, circumstance,* and the like until we formed the image of clashing events. *Irony is the surprise of clashing events.* That got us thinking about irony as the meeting of two events. *Irony is a surprising relationship.*

STEP 4—IN/OF

Follow the *realm word* with *in* or *of*, if applicable.
- Irony is a concurrence *of events . . .*
- A geosyncline is a formation *in the earth . . .*
- Feudalism is a system *of society . . .*
- The prime rate is the rate *of interest . . .*
- Infrastructure is a system *of structures . . .*
- Detoxification is a process *in the liver . . .*

STEP 5—WHICH

Follow the *prepositional phrase* with the word *which* or a *which phrase*, such as *through which, in which, by which, for which,* etc. This sets up transition so that we can bring the term from the realm into the part of the definition where the term is doing some action.
- Irony is a concurrence of events *in which . . .*
- Photosynthesis is a process *in which . . .*
- A geosyncline is a depression in the earth *into which . . .*

- Feudalism is a system of society *in which* . . .
- The prime rate is the rate of interest *which* . . .
- Infrastructure is a system of structures *by which* . . .
- Detoxification is a process in the liver *through which* . . .

STEP 6—ACTION STATEMENT

Follow the *pronoun* or *which phrase* by an *action statement*. In the action statement, something does something to something.

- Irony is a concurrence of events in which *fate turns the tables on our expectations.*
- Photosynthesis is a process in which *plants transform sunlight into food.*
- A geosyncline is a depression in the earth into which *sediments have been deposited over a long period of time.*
- Feudalism is a system of society in which *serfs work the land owned by a lord.*
- The prime rate is a rate of interest which *banks charge their best customers.*
- Infrastructure is a system of structures by which *a city or town connects people across distances.*
- Detoxification is a process in the liver through which *enzymes transform toxins into excretable substances.*

SENTENCE TWO: RIGHT-BRAIN (METAPHORICAL) THINKING

A well-formed definition can't be the end of the story. Having worked so hard on this definition, there must be more juice that we can squeeze out it. Having laid out the details, we can now play. We can play with visualization, metaphor, wordplay, euphony.

The first sentence is deliberate, sober, methodical, and sequential: *left-brained*. The second is whimsical, creative, metaphorical, and lighthearted: *right brained*. Wordplay is at work in each of these second sentences.

- Dynamic word choice: Irony is a surprising *clash* of events.
- Visual image: *Picture a basin* in the earth. As layers of sediment settle in, they sink and compress.
- Comparison: *You can't think of feudalism as a ladder* because you can climb up a ladder. The feudal structure is more like sedimentary rock: what's on the bottom will always be on the bottom unless some cataclysmic event occurs.
- Punning: The *prime* rate is served to the *choicest* customers.

- ♦ Analogy: Infrastructure *is to a city or town what the circulatory system* is to the body.
- ♦ Wordplay: Detoxification makes poisons "kick-outable."

(See Appendix: *Metaphorical Thinking Prompts*.)

COMPONENTS OF THE RIGHT-BRAIN (METAPHORICAL) SENTENCE

The right-brain sentence can use any of the following:

- ♦ Begin with the term itself. This is to create parallel structure (a pattern) between the first and second sentence.
- ♦ Personify the concept: Picture it *doing* something.
- ♦ Use lively language to express what the concept is doing..
- ♦ Use short, strong words as keywords.

SUMMARY

In composing definitions, the first sentence, the *serious* sentence, lays the intellectual groundwork for negotiating the concept; the second sentence, the *fun* sentence, enables the learner to remember it. For the left-brain sentence, we use technical, scholarly language. But for the right-brain sentence, we switch language gears: The simpler the language, the more metaphorical, visual, and memorable the image is likely to be. Either alone is insufficient, but both together combine to form real and lasting learning that results from whole brain thinking.

USING NEW WORDS IN A SENTENCE

When we ask Jamie to use a new word in a sentence, we want her to animate the word by nestling it in a real context. This differs from writing a definition, because a definition is not so much a deployment of the word as it is a clinical denotation of it. So, we instruct the class to write illustrative sentences, and all too often what we get looks something like this:

Industrialized: *China was industrialized.*

Tsarist: *In Russia there were many tsarists.*

Capitalize: *They tried to capitalize.*

This isn't exactly what we had in mind. How can we structure the "use it in a sentence" assessment? We want a sentence that will feature our new word in a starring role, backgrounded by a cast of characters of supportive words which sing and dance obediently behind it.

For students to welcome a new word into their language, they have to use the word in a sentence, and the nature of that sentence has to meet certain criteria.

SOCIAL STUDIES

- ◆ Provide substance: The sentence has to have at least twenty-five words and no redundancies.

- ◆ Provide action: The sentence must be powered by an action word, not *is/was*.

- ◆ Provide a synonym or defining phrase in another part of the sentence so that the sentence clearly illustrates the meaning. A person reading the sentence who is unfamiliar with the word should be able to figure it out. The synonym can be a single word or phrase which acts as a synonym. It has to appear in another part of the sentence so that it isn't just there as a redundancy, but as part of the rich texture of a well-constructed sentence.

- ◆ Provide visuals and details: For the meaning of the word and context to come alive, we need vivid images and specifics.

TIPS

- ◆ Don't rush into it: You don't have to use the word at the beginning of the sentence. Set the stage first.

- ◆ Think of the sentence as a story.

    <u>Obsequious</u>: *Although I tried to stand up to the team captain and not be so timid, I obeyed her orders again like an obsequious puppy at dog training school.*

    <u>Barogram</u>: *After studying the barogram, the meteorologist looked up in alarm, realizing that this air pressure chart indicated that a hurricane was headed straight for his part of town.*

    <u>Illuminated</u>: *Working under a vow of silence, with Gregorian chants resounding off the stone cathedral walls, Medieval monks used gilded brushes to paint elaborate illuminated manuscripts of the Scriptures.*

    <u>Primogeniture</u>: *To subvert the tradition of primogeniture, Prince Edred secretly contemplated killing his older brother Herbert, whose first-born status entitled him to the crown.*

    <u>Proximity</u>: *You're lucky you were nowhere near the doorway when the proximity monitor activated the intruder alarm, spraying a noxious, sticky, hard-to-remove substance within a six-foot perimeter.*

650 VERBS

To understand the verbs is to understand the action. To understand the action is to understand the subject. For this reason, we traffic in verbs. What follows are lists of verbs for various subjects. Students should lean heavily on

INTERDIS-CIPLINARY

these verbs in writing. They will focus the sentence, provide the proper language tone, and cut down on wordiness.

50 VERBS: MATH

Math is a realm of operations, relationships, doing this to that. Math is about making changes, measuring, expanding, and condensing. It is about expressing things in different ways, following procedures, applying formulas.

add	connect	draw	graph	predict
apply	construct	equalize	interpret	represent
arrange	correspond	estimate	intersect	simplify
assign	demonstrate	evaluate	justify	slope
assume	depend	express	match	solve
bisect	designate	extrapolate	measure	subtract
calculate	determine	factor	multiply	substitute
change	differ	find	operate	suppose
coincide	distribute	follow	order	travel
compare	divide	function	plot	vary

50 VERBS: WORLD LANGUAGES

When we learn a new language we use templates. We take a sentence and put it into various tenses. We substitute nouns for other nouns. We learn idiomatic templates that fall into categories such as small talk, finding one's way, making purchases, or ordering at a restaurant. The verbs on this list are the ones learned in the first two years of a new language. With them, we can communicate on a basic level.

act	eat	learn	plan	take
ask	feel	listen	pick	taste
be	find	like	put	think
buy	fix	live	refuse	touch
call	give	look for	say	use
change	go	make	see	wait
come	have	meet	sell	walk
die	help	need	show	want
dislike	hold	offer	speak	work
do	lack	order	stop	understand

50 VERBS: HISTORY

History is about conditions that exist because of geography and natural resources, technology, economics, and leadership. History is the tracking of changes: power struggles, technological developments, natural disasters, and

HISTORY

heroes and monsters. It is about cycles and themes, unintended consequences, and fortuitous accidents.

advance	control	export/import	invade	result
affect	convert	follow	isolate	retreat
attack	decline	force	lead to	rise
begin	demand	form	modernize	rule
believe	develop	govern	practice	support
build	dominate	grow	produce	trade
cause	end	increase/decrease	promote	turn
change	establish	industrialize	rebel	urbanize
conflict	expand	influence	reflect	vanquish
contribute	explore	integrate	reign	worship

50 VERBS: RELIGIOUS STUDIES

RELIGION

Religious studies are about relationships between human beings and the Deity, matters concerning morals and ethics, and living a purposeful life guided by religious precepts.

administer	consecrate	find	observe	ritualize
bestow	contemplate	follow	offer	sacrifice
bless	convert	form	practice	sanctify
build	create	fulfill	praise	seek
care	curse	guide	pray	study
chant	damn	inspire	protect	support
clarify	deliver	lift	purify	teach
cleanse	devote	love	reflect	transcend
condemn	discover	meditate	reach	understand
congregate	establish	minister (to)	reveal	worship

50 VERBS: BUSINESS

BUSINESS

Business has three points: buyer, seller, and product. The language of business is the language of exchange, of movement of goods/services and money, and the machinations attendant upon getting money from one hand to another. Business language is built for speed: we're looking for the unadorned, straightforward sentence.

account for	bill	collect	evaluate	invest
advertise	buy	count	exchange	liquidate
agree	borrow	decline	hire	lose
balance	cash in	decrease	hold	manufacture
bid	close	deduct	increase	negotiate

offer	present	return	settle	supply
order	profit	risk	set up	tender
owe	purchase	save	sign	trade
pay	reduce	sell	spend	transact
pitch	remit	serve	stock	transfer

50 VERBS: GOVERNMENT/POLITICS/LAW

Most of the words of government/politics/law have a Latinate pedigree. These are words about procedures, channels, and authority. They have an imposing, formal air, one worthy of Ionic columns and black robes.

adjudicate	decree	govern	oppose	represent
administrate	defend	impose	oversee	restrain
advocate	deliberate	influence	promote	restrict
agitate	democratize	initiate	propose	rule
arbitrate	deregulate	institute	prosecute	supervise
argue	elect	intervene	pursue	support
assert	empower	investigate	qualify	sustain
campaign	enact	legislate	reform	tyrannize
debate	enforce	lobby	regulate	veto
decide	file	maintain	report	vote

50 VERBS: CHEMISTRY

Chemistry is about why things change and how things interact with each other under a given set of conditions. It is highly classified information. Like earth science, it is about heat, water, motion, pressure, splitting up, and coming together. Like math, it is abstract because the stuff of chemistry has to be composed in our imaginations even though it is real.

absorb	complete	evaporate	level	react
act	contain	exchange	liquefy	release
affect	control	explode	lower	remain
attract	cool	form	maintain	remove
balance	deploy	free	melt	repel
behave	differ	fuse	mix	respond
bond	discharge	heat	occur	saturate
burn	dissolve	implode	oxidize	separate
calculate	equalize	involve	produce	share
change	equate	join	raise	transfer

EARTH SCIENCE

50 VERBS: EARTH SCIENCE

Earth science is about time and change. Whereas chemistry tends to be about rapid, explosive change, earth science is often about slow but dramatic change. But earth science is also about fury: air, earth, water, fire and their Olympian whims. Earth science includes the study of the biosphere and the dynamic equilibrium that supports planetary life.

absorb	cut	erode	moderate	shorten
accumulate	date	fill	move	sift
arrange	decrease	float	originate	sink
build	develop	flow	overturn	spin
cement	disintegrate	form	precipitate	split
change	dissolve	increase	radiate	support
cleave	diverge	intensify	raise	travel
collapse	drift	maintain	reflect	turn
compact	drop	melt	release	weaken
converge	elongate	migrate	settle	weather

BIOLOGY

50 VERBS: BIOLOGY

A student learning biology gets an education in words: prefixes, suffixes, and roots. Biology is a mouthful of interesting words and classifications. Like chemistry and earth science, biology is the study of systems and cycles. In biology, we learn about systems within systems, all overlapping with our knowledge of earth science, chemistry, and physics.

acidify	deoxygenate	expand	interact	pump
act	develop	fertilize	metabolize	react
block	die	filter	mutate	regenerate
breathe	differentiate	flow	nourish	reproduce
connect	digest	function	oxygenate	respond
contract	disperse	graft	perform	secrete
control	divide	hydrate	process	stimulate
cross	evolve	impede	produce	synthesize
decompose	exchange	inflame	proliferate	transmit
dehydrate	excrete	ingest	protect	transport

50 VERBS: PHYSICS

Physics is a force to be reckoned with. It's the study of work, energy, and push versus pull. It's how things move, melt, mesh, burn, break, bounce, rock, roll, and ride. And the best part of physics is that, unlike the microscopic, unreal world of biology and chemistry, unlike the vast universe that is earth science, physics is something you can actually see with your own eyes. It's believable. (some of it.)

act	convert	explode	lower	relay
adhere	counteract	evaporate	measure	repel
attract	deflect	float	meet	reverse
balance	differentiate	flow	melt	rotate
bounce	disengage	fly	pull	signal
burn	draw	force	push	sink
calibrate	drive	gather	raise	spin
cohere	engage	ignite	react	touch
collect	exert	implode	recycle	turn
contract	expand	launch	reflect	vibrate

50 VERBS: LITERATURE

Literature is a subject of following a storyline, understanding characters, and reading between the lines. In literature, language is allowed to meander and secondary stories to intervene. The reader wishes to respond emotionally, and there may well be a parallel meaning constructed in the reader's mind, known as *symbolism*. In literature, words are expected to harmonize in sound and sense, evoking and implying subtle meanings: words come together like colors on the color wheel, forming new meanings in new combinations.

alliterate	connote	explain	juxtapose	represent
ascertain	contrast	explicate	mean	rhyme
analyze	convey	expose	motivate	satirize
begin	denote	express	narrate	specify
characterize	describe	foreshadow	overstate	suggest
clash	dramatize	imagine	personify	summarize
coincide	end	imply	philosophize	symbolize
compare	entail	infer	portray	tie in
conflict	evoke	inform	proceed	translate
connect	exaggerate	interpret	relate	understate

50 VERBS: ART/ART HISTORY

The language of art is similar to that of literature in that the viewer, like the reader, is expected to interpret, to pick up subtle and obvious signals, and to respond emotionally as well as intellectually. A work of art must be considered in terms of its historical context, its literal level, and its relation to the viewer's prior knowledge/experience.

ART/ART HISTORY

adorn	define	fill	lighten	recognize
balance	depict	focus	mark	reflect
comment	distort	highlight	memorialize	repeat
compose	dramatize	idealize	mix	represent
contrast	emphasize	illustrate	obscure	sculpt
convey	enclose	imply	ornament	sharpen
cover	exaggerate	indicate	outline	stroke
cross	exhibit	intensify	overshadow	suggest
crosshatch	express	juxtapose	point to	symbolize
darken	evoke	lead	portray	unify

50 VERBS: MUSIC/MUSIC HISTORY

The language of music often relies on metaphor. We speak of the *color* or *weight* of a particular sound quality because music cannot be described in words. Highly mathematical, music is about patterns and the division of time. People who write about music rely on emotional, lively verbs.

MUSIC/ MUSIC HISTORY

accent	converge	flow	orchestrate	stylize
accompany	counter	harmonize	perform	swing
amplify	croon	hold	pound	syncopate
beat	diverge	improvise	repeat	synchronize
blend	echo	intensify	rest	trill
burst	embellish	interpret	reverberate	tune
chant	energize	intone	rise	vamp
clash	evoke	jam	skitter	vary
compose	express	jump	slide	vocalize
conduct	fall	modulate	soften	wail

USING THE 650 VERBS

Clearly, there is much overlap from one subject to another. This implies that, from one subject to another, similar thinking skills are involved. How can we use these lists?

♦ These lists are arranged alphabetically. How can these terms be categorized?

♦ Add to them, from readings in the textbook and in newspaper articles.

♦ Find two verbs that are similar and explain the difference between them.

♦ Use the verbs of one subject to describe another.

♦ To understand the verbs is to understand the subject. Write sentences for each verb that illustrate your understanding of the subject.

◆ Accurate, interesting writing depends on strong verbs. Although we sometimes have to base a sentence on weak verbs, we should make it a habit to energize our language with as many strong verbs as possible.

◆ By using the verb list for each subject, we employ the proper language tone.

TWO HATS

An educated person knows that the same word can be used one way in ordinary speech and another way in its context as a technical term. Words, like people, play various roles depending on the context. Jamie, with her emergent word sense, needs practice in moving a word from the vernacular to the academic. Just as she is developing more nuanced roles for herself, Jamie is learning something about nuancing and context.

	Mathematics	Vernacular
Acute	The acute angle measures 70 degrees.	Appendicitis can lead to acute pain
Degree	There are 360 degrees in a circle.	My mother needs two more courses for her degree.
Domain	The function of the independent variable and that of the dependent variable are called the range and the domain	My room is a sacred domain that you must only enter with my permission.
Entries	The numbers in a matrix are called entries.	I made three entries in my journal this week.
Factor	Factor the expression.	Weather was a factor in my decision to cancel.
Function	Y is a function of X.	What is the function of this strange device?
Origin	The origin is the point of intersection of two axes.	We traced the point of origin . of the river
Sphere	A sphere is the set of all points in space that are a given distance from a point.	A ball is a sphere.
Value	A value is the given measurement of a quantity.	What is the value of a dollar in Spain?

MATH

The following words are common in the vernacular but wear a special hat when used in chemistry class:

	Chemistry	Vernacular
Indicator	The indicator turned red, signaling the presence of a contaminating substance.	The indicator light on the dashboard indicates that I need oil.
Catalyst	A catalyst accelerates a chemical reaction by lowering activation energy of the reaction.	An crisis is a catalyst for change.
Group	On the Periodic Table, the elements along one column are considered a group.	Group like elements together.
Period	On the Periodic Table, the period number indicates the valence of a given element.	These are the paintings that Picasso created during his Blue Period.
Salt bridge	Ions flow along a salt bridge in an electrochemical cell.	The army ants are building a salt bridge between the sidewalk cracks.
Solution	A solution consists of extremely small particles in a homogenous mixture.	I have found the solution to this problem.

The following words wear one hat for social studies, another for science/math.

	Social Studies	Science
Culture	The culture of the Aztecs included a polytheistic religion.	A tissue sample was cultured in the petri dish to diagnose streptococcus infection.
Axis	In WWII, the Axis Powers were defeated on D-Day.	The Earth rotates on its axis.
Deposition	The witness gave a deposition.	Deposition causes material to migrate.
Atmosphere	The atmosphere promoted nationalism and warfare.	The atmosphere of the Earth is divided into temperature zones.
Front	WWII was fought on two fronts.	There's a cold front headed this way this weekend.
Diffusion	Cultural diffusion is a theme of the twentieth century.	Diffusion is the movement of particles from an area of high concentration to one of low concentration.

SUMMARY

There's more to vocabulary than memorizing lists and matching words with stiff definitions. Each subject area has its own lexicon, but there is a great concurrence of words and roots across the board. To learn words that will stay with us, we need to make connections from one class to another. We also need to mix technical terms with simple, everyday verbs that will make esoteric concepts accessible. Jamie's social studies teacher has done a great job in expanding Jamie's vocabulary with words that she can use not only for social studies but for general communication as well. Jamie's social studies notebook looks like this:

- At least twice weekly, Jamie writes well-developed sentences which use the terminology in context.

- Social studies terms are related to language that Jamie is learning in other classes. In her social studies notebook, Jamie has space to jot down terms from science class which have similar prefixes and roots.

- Jamie develops flexibility and a sense of context. She writes sentences which use her social studies terms in other fields and in the vernacular.

- Jamie's social studies notebook has plenty of lists, and space for expanding these lists. She has lists of verbs, useful phrases around which to build sentences, and specialized terminology. Her lists come from her text and academic readings, as well as outside readings, such as newspaper articles and editorials.

- Words learned are not left behind. Jamie has opportunities and reminders to use words repeatedly once they are learned.

- Jamie writes definitions according to the "whole brain" approach.

- She distinguishes subtle differences between closely related terms.

- She gives examples for terms.

- She is careful to spell terms correctly. Her teacher takes points off for misspellings of social studies terms.

Jamie's notebook is checked and graded at least once each quarter. Her teacher considers completeness, correctness, care in presentation, and evidence that Jamie has done more than just copy off the board.

6

ORGANIZERS
FRAMES, CLUSTERS, AND STEMS

CHAPTER OVERVIEW

One of the purposes of assigning writing tasks is to help students organize and categorize information. In any given unit of study, students need to sort details, establish main ideas, and see connections and patterns. This chapter addresses the following questions:

♦ How can I help students *classify information?*

♦ How can I help students *make comparisons?*

♦ How can I help students name *characteristics* of a concept?

♦ How can I help students write about *chronological* events?

♦ How can I help students *support an assertion?*

♦ How can I help students establish **cause and effect?**

♦ How can I use the patterns that I find in professional writing to help my students be better writers and thinkers in my subject area?

* * *

PATTERNS AND CLUSTERS

Andrew appreciates when his teachers help him see patterns. Every day, his head is crammed with facts and figures, dates, names, places, formulas, arrows, symbols, definitions, maps, diagrams, study guides, instructions, timelines, reference tables, and formulas. His backpack has more names and numbers than the Manhattan phone book. But he's learned to organize and approach information in various clusters, each of which is suited to a learning strategy.

♦ Essential questions

♦ Key words

♦ Paragraph patterns

♦ Sentence stems

CLASSIFICATIONS

We have lots of terminology, and all of it belongs someplace. We're listing, sorting, naming, categorizing, and subordinating. We're making tree diagrams and outlines, headings and subheadings.

ESSENTIAL QUESTIONS

What are the main categories? What are the subcategories, and can these be factored into smaller subcategories? How do the subcategories relate to the main category?

KEY WORDS

breakdown	circuitry	levels	stratification	system
category	hierarchy	network	structure	taxonomy
classification	layers	organization	subcategory	types

PARAGRAPH PATTERN

A paragraph that classifies information will have a series of specialized terms. The series is often introduced by a colon. Typically, the topic sentence will introduce the main category and the subcategories. The supporting sentences will tell the function of the subcategories and may further refine them:

The Nervous System

The nervous system is made up of three types of neurons: sensory neurons, interneurons, and motor neurons. The sensory neurons transmit impulses from receptors to the central nervous system. The central nervous system consists of the brain and spinal cord. The sensory neurons are located mainly in the eyes, ears, tongue, nose, and skin. Interneurons are located mainly in the central nervous system. Their job is to transmit nerve impulses between the sensory and motor neurons. The motor neurons transmit impulses from the central nervous system to effectors. These impulses cause muscles, effectors, and glands to respond. (From Garnsey, Wayne. 1990. Regents Biology Review. Middletown, NY: N & N, p. 101.)

SENTENCE STEMS

- ◆ State the main category in one sentence.
- ◆ Use a colon to present the subcategories as a series.
- ◆ Subcategory #1: State the function and major characteristics.
- ◆ Subcategory #2: State the function and major characteristics.
- ◆ Subcategory #3: State the function and major characteristics.

BIOLOGY

COMPARISONS

We have two versions of something. We're delineating the characteristics of two things and finding similarities. We're considering how two things are alike in structure, application, sequence, cause/effect, and general nature. We're looking for points of convergence and divergence. We're considering which differences are essential and which are superficial.

ESSENTIAL QUESTIONS

What do these two things have in common? How do we know that they are different? Are the differences gross or subtle? Can these two things be considered opposite?

KEY WORDS

as opposed to	different	on the other hand	unlike
but	however	same	variation
compared to	instead of	similar	while

PARAGRAPH PATTERN

The comparison/contrast pattern is a favorite format for essay-writing. The first sentence establishes the main point of comparison. The supporting sentences relate the two subjects to this point of comparison.

Confucianism/Daoism

The two main Chinese religions, Confucianism and Daoism, represent different beliefs about man's place in society and in nature. Confucianists believe in a strong government where the individual is subservient to rulers. They stress social organization and respect for hierarchy over individual rights. On the other hand, Daoists believe in a weak government and stress man's relationship with nature and magic. Confucianists believe that peace is achieved by orderly behavior of individuals who accept their place in society. Daoists believe that peace is achieved by man's immersing himself in nature.

SENTENCE STEMS

♦ Use a semicolon to compare/contrast: _____; _____.

♦ Use a semicolon + a conjunctive adverb (or a transitional expression) to contrast: _____; however, (on the other hand) _____.

♦ Use a comma + conjunction to contrast: _____, but (yet) _____.

♦ Use the both/and structure to compare: Both _____and _____ (have something, do something _____.

RELIGION

CHARACTERISTICS

We have a concept. We're delimiting, drawing boundaries. We're considering the factors that allow us to generalize. We're thinking about the essentials of something, what it is that makes us know what it is.

ESSENTIAL QUESTIONS

What are the attributes of this concept? What is the broadest definition of it? What is the narrowest? What parts comprise it? How do the parts operate with each other to produce the whole?

KEY WORDS

act together	comprise	features	produce	quality
attributes	facet	layout	property	trait
characteristic	factors	mark		

PARAGRAPH PATTERN

This type of paragraph is descriptive, and likely to be arranged in spatial order. The topic sentence presents an overall statement about the whole thing; the supportive sentences present the particulars and the relationship of parts to whole.

Binoculars

A pair of binoculars is basically two small refracting telescopes that together produce a stereoscopic or three-dimensional view. Each eye sees a separate close-up view, but the brain combines them to perceive an image that has depth. Binoculars have prisms. The objective lens gives an upside down reversed image. The first prism reverses this image again so that it appears the right way around, and the second prism inverts it so that the image is upright. (From Macaulay, D. 1988. *The Way Things Work.* Boston: Houghton-Mifflin, p 202.)

SENTENCE STEMS

- ♦ A (whole _____ consists of (a) _____which serves to _____.
- ♦ The purpose of the (part) is to _____.
- ♦ (Part) and (part) work together to _____.

CHRONOLOGY

We have a sequence. We're understanding something in terms of time, putting things in time order.

ESSENTIAL QUESTIONS

What happens when? How does something develop over time? Can the sequence be taken out of order? Would the outcome be different if the sequence were reversed at any point?

KEY WORDS

before/after	final	later	procedure	then
chronological	first, second, etc.	lead to	process	time
events	last	order	sequence	turn into

PARAGRAPH PATTERN

Whether an anecdote or a procedural report, the chronology pattern takes us through things in the order in which they happen. Although literature often mixes up the sequence for dramatic effect, academic writing is straightforward: first things happen first.

The Rise of Napoleon

Napoleon's rise to glory came early in the French Revolution. He drove out the British forces from Toulon in late 1793. He then savored victories over the Hapsburgs. In 1798 he led a flamboyant expedition into Egypt for the purpose of foiling British trade with India. This venture was less than successful, but Napoleon managed to conceal its failure from his countrymen. Beginning in 1799, his strategy was to appropriate grand titles for himself, including First Consul, consul for life, and, finally, in 1804, Emperor of the French.

SOCIAL STUDIES

SENTENCE STARTERS

♦ First, _____.

♦ Then, _____.

♦ After that, _____.

CLAIMS AND CASES

We have an assertion. We're supporting, proving, verifying, justifying.

ESSENTIAL QUESTIONS

How can we prove our claim? What are the counterarguments? How can we refute them? How strong is our conviction toward this claim? What is empirical? hypothetical? theoretical? experiential? anecdotal? What experts do we rely on?

KEY WORDS

assert	claim	factual	proven	support
believe	declare	propose	statistical	theory

SOCIAL STUDIES

PARAGRAPH PATTERN

The first sentence makes an assertion, a claim that has to be proven. The supportive sentences provide reasons, examples and facts which back up the assertion.

> I believe that although Harry S. Truman was controversial in his own time, he maintains a place of honor in history as one of the strongest, most decisive Presidents of the twentieth century. Truman ended World War II by his decision to drop the atom bomb on Hiroshima and Nagasaki in August, 1945. He desegregated the army. He fired Douglas MacArthur. Truman believed that Communism was a deadly threat and he instituted several programs which halted the spread of Communism in Europe: NATO, the Marshall Plan, and the Truman Doctrine.

SENTENCE STEMS

♦ Assertion: (a direct, simple claim:
   I believe that _____.

♦ Support:
   Example 1: _____.
   Example 2: _____.
   Example 3: _____.

CAUSES, CONSEQUENCES, AND CONDITIONS

We have an action and reaction. We're thinking about why something happens, what follows from what. We're predicting, explaining, and reasoning.

ESSENTIAL QUESTIONS

What will happen because of what? Is there a single cause or multiple causes? Will the same result always follow the same cause?

KEY WORDS

accordingly	consequence	for this reason	lead to	therefore
because	effects of	if . . . then	result	thus

PARAGRAPH PATTERN

The cause/effect paragraph can open with a question as its topic sentence. The supportive sentences present the various factors that answer this question.

> What caused the fall of Rome? One cause was political: the government lost popular support because of its oppressive policies, widespread corruption, and in-fighting. Military causes included sloppy, disloyal armies, weakened by Germanic invasions. Social causes were a decline in population due to war and disease, a weakening of patriotism and the excesses of the rich.

SOCIAL STUDIES

Economic causes were excessive taxes, slave labor and indenture of farmers to the landowners. General demoralization and lack of discipline affected every aspect of life in the Roman empire and led to its collapse.

SENTENCE STEMS

- Question about cause/effect _____?
- Example 1: _____.
- Example 2: _____.
- Example 3: _____.

CRITICISMS

We have an emotional or intellectual response. We're evaluating, weighing, accepting/rejecting, establishing criteria, and judging something against them.

ESSENTIAL QUESTIONS

What are the criteria? Where does this subject stand in terms of the criteria? Is my response emotional or intellectual? How can I separate the emotional from the intellectual? How do I establish the credibility of my sources?

KEY WORDS

according to	clear	effective	less/more than	power
as much as	compared to	is considered	not as	reach

PARAGRAPH PATTERN

The topic sentence establishes the subject and our response to it. Supportive sentences justify our opinion.

> *I think the 1965 Supreme Court case "Tinker v. Des Moines" would make a good movie. The case is about two teenagers, John and Mary Beth Tinker, who wore black armbands to school to protest the Vietnam War. When they were suspended for doing this, they sued, and the case went to the Supreme Court. In 1969 The Supreme Court ruled in favor of the Tinkers. The case would make an interesting movie because the subject is considered important and controversial. It deals with basic civil rights and the conflict between students and school officials.*

SENTENCE STEMS

- I think _____ because _____ is considered _____ because _____.

How can Andrew use this information about patterns? He can move around a topic, examining it from each of the above perspectives, deciding which ones apply to a topic and which do not. He can use the key words and

SOCIAL STUDIES

sentence stems to organize his thinking and to structure clear sentences. Patterning leads to orderly thinking, efficient habits of mind, and organized note-taking.

4Cs: SENTENCE STEMS

- **Template: Comparison:** A is/has/does more/less than B.

    Sweden has less daylight than Canada but Swedes spend less of their income on energy costs than Canadians do.

- **Template: Concession:** Even though (although, despite, though) A exists, B exists.

    Even though Sweden is more northerly than Canada, the climate of Sweden not much colder than Canada because Sweden is warmed by the North Atlantic Drift.

- **Template: Condition:** If or unless A exists, then B will exist.

    If air is cooled below dewpoint temperature, then moisture in the air will condense.

- **Template: Concurrence:** As A is going on in the background, B is going in the foreground.

    As heat and pressure cause the minerals in rock to melt, metamorphic rocks form out of these minerals.

SENTENCE STEMS: THIS/THAT

- The variation in THIS suggests THAT.
- The evidence of THIS implies THAT.
- If THIS, then THAT because . . .
- Since THIS ,we get THAT because . . .
- THIS represents THAT.
- THIS is/are caused by THAT.
- THIS causes THAT because . . .
- THIS is associated with THAT.
- The (more/less) THIS, the more/less THAT.
- THIS is likely to bring about THAT.

PARAGRAPH PATTERNS IN THE NEWSPAPER

What follows are some paragraph patterns and explanations of how to recognize them. *The New York Times*, on any given day, will have representative samples in its various sections.

Pattern	Features	Newspaper Section
Development by facts	Statistics, place names, names of people, scientific principles	News reports Business analysis
Development by examples	Series, concrete details	Editorials
Development by reasons	Because, cause/effect statements	Reviews: books, music, theater, film
Development by incident	Time cues, descriptions of people, beginning/middle/end	Feature stories
Development by images and sensory details	References to physical sensations	Food Sports

SUMMARY

Skilled readers and writers rely on organizational patterns to hold information together. To become better writers, students need to be mindful of textual patterns in their readings. Graphic organizers can help the student make the leap from skillful reading to skillful writing.

Noting organizational patterns helps the student to

♦ Connect learning from one topic to another and from class to class.

♦ Discern main information from subordinate information.

♦ Discern sequences.

♦ Make predictions.

♦ Recall and locate information.

Graphic organizers can be used to review, to prepare for writing, and to check writing. Students can use teacher-generated graphic organizers, or they can devise their own formats.

PART II

APPLICATIONS

7

RESEARCH PAPERS AND WEBQUESTS

ABOUT RESEARCH PAPERS

The research paper is the queen of the academic writing genres. She is an exacting queen who rules from afar, and whose rules pass through many members of court before reaching down to her timorous subjects. In this chapter, I define the term *research paper* and explain why some of the problems we have with it can be solved through staff development to draw up a scope and sequence.

Information about the steps of the research process and style guides is readily available in profusion. I've sought not to duplicate such information, but rather to address concerns that English teachers and teachers of other subject areas have as they assign and assess the traditional research paper.

The WebQuest is the modern, more lively form of the research paper. The last part of this chapter explains what WebQuests are, what their value is, where to find ready-to-go ones, and how to set up your own.

WHAT IS A RESEARCH PAPER?

The terms *research paper* and *term paper* are often used as though they are synonyms. They aren't. However, in any given faculty, especially on the K-12 level, we are likely to have teachers who don't recognize a difference; we need to keep the conflation of terms in mind as we communicate with students. Even if we work in a school that has a common lexicon, we still have students coming in from other schools who have different models in mind when they hear of a particular academic genre. The important thing is that students know what we want and understand that we are the audience and that we have certain expectations. Regardless of the terminology used by colleagues, we must make our expectations explicit.

A research paper is a formal academic genre that requires the writer to adhere to certain formats, depending on the subject area. The writer states a thesis and then integrates information from outside sources with his or her own knowledge and opinions to bring the thesis to a conclusion. In a research paper, the writer makes an assertion (research) and then goes about bolstering that assertion with information from credible outside sources, giving weight and academic backing to the argument. The reader expects the writer to give due credit to the outside sources.

The reader expects the writer to reveal critical thinking and due respect for academic traditions. By the former, I mean that the writer has to do more than just summarize or paraphrase what experts have to say. By the latter, I mean that the writer has to conform to the detailed structure of citations set forth by an academic institution, usually MLA or APA, but sometimes CBE, Chicago Manual of Style, or COS (Columbia Online Style). Teachers specify which of these styles they want, and teachers should teach, or at least review and show a model of, papers in that style.

Let me go back a bit: Students do need to know how to summarize and paraphrase before they can write a decent research paper. The academic term for a paper that summarizes and paraphrases existing information is "review of the literature." Students do need to understand the difference between "review of the literature" and the critical thinking (analysis and argumentation) skills necessary for more sophisticated research papers. Many teachers expect a "review of the literature" to appear, labeled as such, as part of an analysis or argument.

Tell your students that they are writing a research paper in order to become smarter about a subject and then to express what they've learned, how they've learned it, and what it means. Doing a research paper qualifies them to participate in a serious, creditable conversation: "I know about this. I wrote a research paper on it."

ANALYSIS OR ARGUMENT

We have two major categories of research papers: analysis and argument. Let's use the example of stem cell research as our hypothetical topic for a research paper.

First of all, the writer has to narrow the topic. A good way to do this is to formulate a question that invites critical thinking. To invite critical thinking, the writer must formulate a question that transcends the "What is it?" level:

♦ Are all kinds of stem cell research equally controversial?

♦ What are the arguments for and against stem cell research?

♦ What are the positions of the senators in your state regarding stem cell research?

♦ What is your opinion about federal funding for stem cell research?

The first three questions above are analytical. The last is argumentative. Although students need to learn how to argue, they must first know how to analyze. Analysis is the process of breakdown, understanding, and reorganization.

The writer has to find the discrete components of the issue. Then she has to understand not only what the components are but also how they affect the whole. Finally, she has to reveal new or stronger understandings that she has gained from the process of analyzing the issue.

Analysis of an issue can include its history and development. If you were to analyze stem cell research, you would find answers to these questions?

+ What is stem cell therapy? (In answering this question, you would have to use the technical lexicon that attends to it.)

+ How does stem cell therapy differ from other kinds of therapies for the same diseases?

+ What kinds of scientists believe that stem cell therapy has promise? Are these kinds of scientists credible?

The first step, then, is to formulate a question that you need outside information to explore. The second step is to review some literature. The third step is to lay out the components of the issue, examine them, and then put them back together in your own words. Stopping here would yield an analytical paper. To go to the next step would be to express an informed opinion, an opinion that is fortified by outside sources and an analytical mindset. Argument can be set forth by infusing one's opinion throughout the paper or by taking an objective stance throughout most of the paper, and then asserting one's opinion at the end.

Argumentation, because it calls for evaluation, is more sophisticated than analysis. Analysis, because it calls for restructuring, is more sophisticated than reviewing the literature. Many students at the pre-college level are simply not ready to tackle all three of these modes at once. You may want to differentiate instruction by giving tiered tasks.

Argumentation in a research paper should be tempered. Establish the difference between argumentation and polemic: Polemic is the extreme form of argumentation. The polemicist uses emotional rhetoric and incendiary images to pull an audience into his orbit. Popular movie-makers and radio talk-show hosts are polemicists that students will readily know, but they are likely to think that these polemicists display the kind of rhetoric that you want in an argument. This is the opportunity to teach how choice of detail, diction, anecdote, and overall language tone contribute to how seriously the reader is going to take the writer.

To craft argument, you must set forth pertinent generalizations. You must then support these generalizations with evidence. The evidence can consist of cases, trends, statistics, observations, and anecdotes. You must convince the reader that your support logically connects to your generalizations. All the while, you must maintain the kind of stance, a personal ethic, that allows the reader to trust your motives and information. Argument can have an emotional component. Indeed, any argument on stem cell research *must* have an emotional component because the subject is about quality-of-life and life-and-death matters.

Argumentation can be subtle or implied. A paper about the possibilities of stem cell therapy can be quite persuasive without the writer ever having to get up on a soapbox to support federal funding for research. An overall optimism and enthusiasm for the topic can be just as persuasive as overt endorsements.

It is worthwhile to ask the students to think about their relationship to the topic, to define that relationship as objective or subjective. This relationship will affect diction; diction will affect tone.

SCIENCE RESEARCH VS. HUMANITIES RESEARCH

Research for science classes differs from research for humanities classes. The former is primary research; the latter, secondary research. In doing science research, the student goes about gathering data, analyzing it, and drawing conclusions. The student in an English or history class is going about a very different process: reviewing commentary that already exists in the scholarly literature.

In going about the process of scientific research, the student records her steps as she makes observations. To be valid, the research process must follow accepted protocols, such as posing a hypothesis, recording results, and drawing conclusions. But the humanities student is not doing the same thing at all. She asks a question and finds out what the scholars think. Whereas the science student is a discoverer, the humanities student is an explorer.

When we ask a science student to write a "research paper," we expect her to conduct an experiment under conventional circumstances and write up her findings in a conventional way, which includes, among other things, an abstract and a review of the literature. When we ask a humanities student to write a "research paper," we expect her to advance her knowledge by adding to it the informed and sophisticated commentary of respected experts.

STYLE GUIDES

Can you blame students for being confused by the different style guides? Why can't there be just one in the world?

Why are there so many style guides? I explain it this way: Let's say you have a university. The university consists of several colleges. We will call them houses, like frat houses. (I like to use the term *house* rather than *college* because high school students, and certainly middle school students, don't really understand how a university is put together with several colleges.) There's a House of the Humanities, a House of the Social Sciences, a House of History, a House of Physical Sciences and Mathematics. Each of these houses has its own interests in terms of what they want to know about where you found your information.

The House of Humanities prefers a style called *MLA*, which stands for Modern Language Association. The key distinguishing features of MLA style are parenthetical citations that provide the author and page. Full citations are provided in the bibliography, which is called *Works Cited*. (The terms *References* or *Bibliography* may also be used.)

The House of Social Sciences prefers a style called *APA*, which stands for American Psychological Association. This style uses parenthetical documentation, but includes the author and the date (year) of publication. This is because the date of publication of information is important to the reader of a social science paper. The reader wants to know how recent the information is because the field is growing constantly.

The House of Physical Sciences and Mathematics also prefers parenthetical citations that give author and date, but this house may prefer a style called *CBE*, which stands for Council of Biology Editors.

Now we come to a small house, the House of History. There are teachers who refer to themselves as history teachers as opposed to those who refer to themselves as social studies teachers. History teachers tend to favor the footnote-endnote style of citation rather than parenthetical citations. Their preferred style guide is *The Chicago Manual of Style*, 14th ed. (Chicago, University of Chicago Press, 1993). Here is where confusion comes in, for students with an incomplete understanding of style guides might want to play it so safe that they include *both* parenthetical citations *and* footnoted ones.

There's even a rising star called *COS*, for Columbia Online Style. This style guide is specifically designed for citing electronic sources.

FORMAL VOICE

Most teachers expect the student to use a formal voice in a research paper. Some of the features of formal voice apply to almost all writing, such as keeping verb tense consistent and using active voice unless one has a reason. Other features are more stodgy than one would usually expect to find in a more reader-friendly genre. Contractions give writing a conversational, inviting tone; but contractions are unwelcome in a formal research paper. We often read the one-sentence paragraph on respectable editorial pages, but not in formal research papers. Acronyms may be used if they are spelled out the first time. Slang or a conversational, breezy tone is to be eschewed, as are stylistic fragments.

Readers of formal research papers expect a third person perspective, and some readers are especially rankled by any lapses into first or second person, even in argumentation. The writer's credibility may be seriously compromised by hedgers such as "in my opinion." The paper should be comprised of formally-developed paragraphs with topic sentences. Lists and bullets are usually eschewed.

Equipping Students with Skills for College Writing

Of course, when we hand students their diplomas with pomp and circumstance, we should be handing them assurance that they will know what to do when given a formal research paper assignment in college. This means that they know how to show a strong organizational structure, with all of its parts well-developed and establishing reader expectation. They should know how to compose operational definitions of key terms; how to use direct, unpadded, but academic language; and how to maintain an objective relationship to the subject.

As you read this, you may be hearkening back to some research papers you've read. You may be thinking that many of your students don't come close to these standards of formality. You may have to lower the temperature a bit to address the real lapses that you find. Whenever possible, give instructional advice in positive language (do's rather than don't's).

1. Refer to people by their first and last names or by their last names.
2. Use as few pronouns, especially "they" and "it," as possible.
3. Begin and end your sentences with strong words.
4. Remember that there is supposed to be a difference between the way you speak and the way you write.
5. Remember that a formal research paper is supposed to have more serious language than other kinds of writing.
6. Every paragraph should be several sentences long.
7. Remember that "formal" means "having form." Just as a tuxedo has more form than a tee shirt, a formal research paper has more sections in it, and is put together with more attention to detail, than other kinds of writing.
8. Use parallel structure as much as possible.
9. Give your paper visual symmetry. Make most paragraphs the same approximate length.
10. Use the kinds of words that you hear your teacher use.
11. Work from an outline.
12. Follow the details of the style guide exactly. Your reader will notice if you make up your own style, such as numbering bibliographic entries. (No style numbers bibliographic entries.)

Redundancy vs. Rhetorical Repetition

Students are very concerned with reaching the required quantity. They simply don't have enough to say. To bridge the gap, they pad. To discourage padding, you warn them not to be repetitious. Nevertheless, I've said before in this book that repetition is an expected and important quality of all communication, including formal research papers. In fact, the very formality of the paper requires repetition. Repetition acts as a motif that strengthens the paper and guides the reader. It's the defining characteristic of coherence.

To teach students the important difference between redundancy and repetition, explain what some English teachers call the *given/new principle*. According to this principal of textual cohesion, the subject of a sentence should state information that has already been given to the reader. The predicate then adds new information, and so on, to form the given/new pattern of delivering information to the reader. We can then explain that repetition in the subject of a sentence is a way to keep the reader's feet on familiar ground. But if there's no new information in the sentence at all, then why should the reader read it? (Certain sentences and paragraphs do give summaries, but the reader is expecting those to appear in conventional places.) Rhetorical repetition helps the reader; redundancy stalls the reader. Rhetorical repetition clarifies and reinforces; redundancy frustrates. Rhetorical repetition brings points into sharper focus; redundancy blurs the message. Students should think in terms of developing paragraphs rather than reaching a certain number of words. The writing task will go faster that way, and the paragraphs will be more meaningful.

THE CHALLENGES

"They didn't answer the question."

"I'm seeing so much plagiarism."

"These papers are so puny. I asked for five to seven pages. Some of these aren't even half that."

"They're using all kinds of abbreviations. It's like they think they're sending a text message. Don't these kids know how to write a paper?"

"This one doesn't even have a Works Cited page. Don't they know you need a Works Cited page?"

If the above expressions of frustration don't hit home, you can skip this part. But if they do reflect your disappointing experience reading research papers, you might want to look closely at where your students actually are in their academic development when you assign a research paper.

A person's development as a writer comes in stages. Writing, unlike speech, is an artificial construct of civilization. People will not come by it naturally. They learn through models, wise directions, and explicit instruction. If you haven't provided these three things, don't assume that someone else has. The task takes informed, persistent effort by English teachers, other subject area teachers, and students.

First, consider the multi-step process of writing a research paper. How many students think they can put it together at the final hour? How many aren't ready to hand the project in by the due date, and then scramble (or take their sweet time) to patch something together days or weeks later? How many are absent on the due date, hastily stretching a few paragraphs into something that might pass for five pages?

If you want success, you need to assist students with their time management. Sketch out interim due dates for outlines, notecards, and drafts. You don't necessarily have to collect these, as you would be stalling the process while you read them; instead, just check off whether they've been completed and open some class time for questions, modeling, and exchanges.

Keep parents informed. The best way to do this is through your class Website. Parents should have the assignment, interim dates, and rubric. They should know the penalties for lateness. (A few parents will enable their children to miss deadlines. There's not much you can do about this.) Be meticulous about your own spelling and grammar in the directions and in all of your communications. Inform parents when interim deadlines have not been met. Set up after school workshops, but don't turn the workshops into tutorials or editing sessions. Have two or three topics, keyed to your rubric.

Districts that are really serious about having students learn to write research papers have a scope and sequence that extends from late elementary grades through high school.

DEVELOPING THE FORMAL ACADEMIC VOICE

One of the biggest problems that students have with research papers is writing in the formal voice. College students and adult writers have difficulty with this skill as well, often forcing a pseudo-intellectual verbiage that is marked by such empty language as "at this point in time" and "the indicators indicate that . . ." George Orwell warned us against language which seeks to prevent, rather than promote, communication.

First, understand that a formal academic voice in writing takes time to develop, and not too many people ever achieve effectiveness or conciseness in this genre. That is not to imply that such a voice is "bad," merely that it is not natural and seldom taught. For it must be learned and practiced. As with any affectation, the novice is going to be halting at first.

It is the English teacher's job to teach students to transit from an informal to a formal voice register. The very ability to do that is a defining characteristic of an educated person. So it stands to reason that we do have to *educate* students to do this.

I have a problem here: I recognize that students must write formal research papers and that these papers must be presented in a formal academic voice. I recognize that our job as teachers is to initiate the novice into the professional conversation, to build layers of language that transcend the language that they already come to school with. But if we demand a formal academic voice without teaching its features and without understanding how language develops, we are asking students to run before they can walk. For some inexplicable reason, we've expected students to learn a manner of using language that they hardly ever encounter, even when reading a drily written textbook. Let's look at the problem of poor academic voice from the perspective of cognitive development.

Writing is not speech on paper, but many poor writers think it is. Who can blame them? They're still new at this thing called writing. They are at the stage where their writerly voices are only just emerging as distinct from their speaking voices. This means, developmentally, that they are nowhere near ready to write in the formal academic voice of a research paper. For many students, the proximal skill is to eliminate those features of speech that are not welcome in writerly prose. If you look at anchor papers representing substandard writing skills, you'll find many "speechisms" that the writer needs to re-form into writerly language. Such students will write "Say you have . . ." when they present an example; they have difficulty deciding where one sentence ends and another begins; they are unsteady in their point of view, jumping around from "I" to "you" with a smattering of "one." They insert informal expressions where they don't belong. But they think expressions like "due to the fact that" and "in the way that" sound smart.

We need to understand what is involved, cognitively, in the development of a new voice, especially for students who have barely achieved the writerly voice on any level. It's a matter of enlightening the teachers about the nature of gradual improvements and how to effect them. I am suggesting that teachers (1) understand that students need explicit instructions to develop the writerly voice and (2) show patience as students try out their new voices. I am suggesting that teachers abide by a 4-12 scope and sequence model that takes students gently through the developmental process of learning to write a research paper. I'm suggesting that the English teacher take the responsibility for teaching the academic voice while teachers of other subject areas assign research projects that are in keeping with the scope and sequence, and not ahead of it. Ideally, staff development should focus on English teachers first, building awareness of the writer's developmental processes and crafting a 4-12 scope and sequence model that comports with it. Then, the second phase of the staff development should be educating teachers in other subject areas about what can reasonably be expected at each grade level.

We have three modes, which work together, of teaching writing:

1. **We read and analyze models.** When we read enough models, our minds latch on to the sentence structure and diction of the genre, and we gradually become able to emulate the prose style.

2. **We teach explicitly.** We explain the difference between formal and informal voice, using the latter to teach the former. We teach rules

that govern all writing and rules that govern the genres. We equip students with vocabulary inventory and sentence templates.

3. **We offer opportunities for practice.** We give constructive feedback and opportunity to apply what has been learned through practice.

The harm in giving students research assignments that demand a writing skill beyond their evolution as writers is twofold: The students not only will become discouraged because of the teacher's frustration, but also will be denied the instruction they need to nurse their voices along naturally. They may grow up to be the kind of bureaucrats that Orwell inveighed against.

Is it any wonder that plagiarism is rampant, given the way we expect students to write? Not only is the formal academic voice beyond them, so that they couldn't write that way if they tried, but there are thousands of research papers for sale on the Internet. If you have an unrealistic expectation about your students' ability to write in a formal academic tone, how are you going to recognize plagiarism when you see it? Fortunately, services such as Turnitin.com (www.turnitin.com) are excellent at detecting plagiarism, but if the student who plagiarized did so because he has no academic voice, what then?

If you are an English teacher, you are in a good position to gauge the academic maturation of your students as displayed in their writing style. Does the student reveal immaturity by using "speechisms" and few "writerisms"? Then that student is not ready to jump to formal academic voice. But what if his economics teacher has assigned a lengthy research paper? And if you are the economics teacher and your department expects such a paper, what do you do? Writing-readiness has to be a schoolwide concern with vigorous administrative support and vision.

The table that follows (see facing page) is a scope and sequence model for writing research papers, grades 4-12. This model carefully takes the academic maturation process into consideration.

SCOPE AND SEQUENCE MODEL FOR WRITING RESEARCH PAPERS
GRADES 4-12

	The student demonstrates competency in the following skills:
Grade 4	Summarizing fact-based written material from a single source
Grade 5	Paraphrasing fact-based written material from a single source Putting together a summary of fact-based information that comes from two sources
Grade 6	Putting together a summary of fact-based information that comes from two sources; paraphrased information included, with running acknowledgement Building a rudimentary bibliography of print and online sources for a topic

SCOPE AND SEQUENCE MODEL FOR WRITING RESEARCH PAPERS
GRADES 4-12 (CONTINUED)

	The student demonstrates competency in the following skills:
Grade 7	Understanding how to cite direct quotations through either running acknowledgement, in-text citation, or footnotes
Grade 8	Understanding that paraphrased information needs to be cited if it is not common knowledge Integrating sourced information (summary, paraphrase, and direct quotations) with original commentary in a report of not more than one page with a simple bibliography and in-text citations; use of running acknowledgement as well as in-text citations
Grade 9	Writing a scaled-down version of an analytical paper, using a given list of sources
Grade 10	Writing a scaled-down version of an argumentation paper, using a given list of sources
Grade 11	Writing a full-scale documented analytical paper that conforms to a major style guide Demonstrating an understanding that different style guides exist for different disciplines at the university level
Grade 12	Writing a full-scale documented argumentation paper that conforms to a major style guide Demonstrating an understanding of differences among the five major style guides: MLA, APA, Chicago, CBE, COS

It's easy to be overly ambitious when it comes to research papers. We may overlook the developmental processes and think that everyone should be able to produce a full-scale, ten-page, fully-documented research paper by the ninth grade. I know of institutions that claim bragging rights to seventh graders who are supposedly composing research treatises of upwards of twenty pages. I wouldn't be impressed by this, unless I saw the results, if I were you. A more prudent plan, and one more likely to lead to actual success in developing writers, is a scope and sequence model that layers skills one year at a time.

Enacting the scope and sequence model is a school-wide job, extending beyond the English teacher's classroom. English teachers need to address other genres of writing in addition to research. Content area teachers have narrower needs in terms of student writing.

SKILL-BUILDERS

We can adhere to a scope and sequence model that gradually introduces the formal research paper without abandoning challenging research tasks that are developmentally appropriate.

Children in the upper elementary grades through high school can write annotated bibliographies, create Hotlists, and follow through on the steps of a WebQuest.

Putting together a Works Cited page, or even including parenthetical citations, is a detail-oriented job. Yet students are not likely to be invested in the importance of the details. Very few people are. It's easy to say, "Who really cares if every entry in the Works Cited page ends with a period?" or "So what if the period is placed after the last word of the sentence rather than outside the parentheses?" I suppose we could just say that following a specified set of directions has intrinsic value. True enough, but in addition to the imperative of "getting things right," learning proper formatting will save time in the long run. Our students' academic and perhaps professional futures will include documentation, so while they are going to the trouble of writing a research paper, we might as well train them in the habit of mind of attending to detail if for no other reason than that doing so is just a good habit.

But you will concede that English teachers are going to care about these conventions more than teachers of other subjects. You may also concede that not all teachers know the rules well enough to feel confident in teaching them. We offer the following four skill builders, two of which are accessible on Quia.com (www.quia.com). Quia.com is a Web-based collection of short answer quizzes and word games.

I call these skill builders "Learning Curves." Each Learning Curve gives the student hands-on practice attending to the details of one part of the research paper process.

LEARNING CURVE 1
ORGANIZATION OF THE WORKS CITED PAGE

Situation: Chrysanthemum had her Works Cited page all set up, and then along came a tsunami and blew it all around. Help Chrysanthemum reorganize her Works Cited page by writing the parts in the proper order for each entry:

City of publication	Title of Book	Date of publication	Author	Publisher

Magazine	Page	Date	Name of article	

Date	Author	Magazine	Page	Name of article

URL	Date of access	Author	Title	Date of publication

URL	Date of access	Date of publication	Title	

LEARNING CURVE 2
PUNCTUATION OF THE WORKS CITED PAGE

Situation: Astor was almost finished with his Works Cited page when a monsoon swept over his village, washing away his punctuation. Help Astor replace the punctuation in the following entries. The first is for a book; the second, a magazine article; the third, an article from the Internet:

Galbraith John The Monsoon Gardener New York Houghton Mifflin Co 2003

The Office of the Future Business Weekly 30 June 2004 48

Lewin Tamar How Tamar Got Her Groove Back 18 Apr 2004 21 May 2004 httpwwwnytimescom

LEARNING CURVE 3
WHAT GOES WITH WHAT?

Situation: Mortimer was talking on his cell phone, drinking a crushed iced caramello latte and resetting the timer on his TIVO remote when his teacher was explaining how to write a research paper. As a result, Mortimer got some of the details mixed up. Answer the following questions for Mortimer:

- ♦ Does the parenthetical citation go before the quote, after the quote, or at the end of the paper?
- ♦ Do I need a Works Cited page *and* a Bibliography page?
- ♦ Am I supposed to number the entries in my Works Cited page?
- ♦ Do I have to put quotation marks around paraphrased information?

♦ Do I need a parenthetical citation after paraphrased information that is not common knowledge?

♦ I read a magazine article while I was getting a haircut that would be perfect for my paper. If I cite this article, do I need to include the date that I got my haircut?

♦ While I was waiting for my girlfriend to get her pedicure finished, I went online on my blackberry and found a great site that would be perfect for my paper. I want to cite it, but I can't remember if her pedicure was last Tuesday or Wednesday? Does it make a difference?

♦ I'm noticing that my research paper has citations in almost every single paragraph. Can that be right?

♦ OK, I'm doing the parenthetical citation thing, right? Where do I put the period from the end of the sentence that the parenthetical citation is for?

♦ Is there any difference between a parenthetical citation and internal documentation?

♦ I'm writing a paper for my bio class. Does that mean I should use the MLA style, or that APA thing, or that other thing, the CBE style? Should I just ask my teacher which one she wants?

♦ Uh-oh! I think I forgot to number the entries on my Works Cited page. Should I ask for my paper back and take the late penalty?

♦ Uh-oh! I think I forgot to end each entry with a period on my Works Cited page. Do you think I'll get points off?

♦ It doesn't make any difference the order that you put the stuff in the Works Cited page entries, as long as it's all there, right?

♦ I'm confused. Sometimes, in the parenthetical citations, I'm seeing the author and the page, but other times I'm seeing the author and the date. What's up with that?

LEARNING CURVE 4
TITLES

Situation: Saturnicus has the annoying habit of underlining and italicizing and placing quotation marks around every title that he writes. Please clarify the rules of title-writing for Saturnicus:

♦ First of all, we do *only one* of the following things: underlining, italicizing, placing quotation marks.

♦ Secondly, underlining and italicizing are interchangeable; you would never do both. You would do one or the other.

♦ Third, we underline titles to indicate that they are full length works. This would include magazines, whole books, movies.

◆ Fourth, we place titles within quotation marks to indicate that they are short works. This would include articles, chapters, poems, Web-sites, and other short works or segments.

Help Saturnicus write the following titles correctly:

◆ Film: The American Presidency

◆ Novel: The American Presidency

◆ A Review That Was Printed in a Magazine: Why The American Presidency Gets My Vote

◆ A Poem: Ode to The American Presidency

FIVE WAYS TO ELIMINATE PLAGIARISM

It's ironic. Although the Internet makes plagiarism incredibly easy to do, the same Internet makes plagiarism easier than ever before to detect and even prevent. Here are two ways to detect plagiarism, and three ways to prevent it.

◆ **Turnitin.com. (www.turnitin.com):** This is a subscriber service for schools or individual teachers. If you subscribe, your students can submit their papers to the service before you read it. The service returns the paper with any verbatim blocks color-coded. The service also archives the papers submitted to prevent students from using each other's papers in the future. Turnitin.com also offers other services to teachers, including an online peer review system and digital portfolios.

◆ **Regular search engines:** Just run a search on a series of words that you think have been lifted verbatim.

◆ **Avoid ready-made tasks:** The more your task asks for text-to-world and text-to-self connections, the less likely it is to be plagiarized.

◆ **Set up checkpoints to show process:** You decrease the risk of all-out plagiarism if you demand to see notes, outlines, sample paragraphs, and other signs that the work is in progress.

◆ **Reward documented paraphrases and summaries:** Build in extra points for properly documented segments. The student must produce the original.

RxRESEARCH

Teaching the research paper is no easy task. You don't just "go over" it in broad strokes and expect students to produce a flawless paper. Students need practice in the discrete parts of the paper. For this reason, I have created a Website that I call RxResearch. It is accessible at:

http://teacherweb.com/NY/HendrickHudsonHighSchool/Mrs Benjamin/index.html

RxResearch links to informative sites as well as the "learning curve" lessons above.

WEBQUESTS: INFORMATION ADVENTURES

WebQuests are investigative activities that are Internet based. There are tons of excellent, peer-reviewed, educator-created WebQuests at:

www.webquest.org

www.filamentality.com

www.webquestdirect.com (a subscriber service)

www.web-n-flow.com

www.discoveryschool.com

The WebQuest idea was created by Bernie Dodge and Tom March out of San Diego State University. Kathy Schrock at Discovery School is another rich vein of information about WebQuesting.

The WebQuest paradigm improves the directions for writing a research paper. Unlike the traditional research paper, the WebQuest points the students to the sources that will yield the targeted information. When we set students loose on the Internet, we often find to our dismay that they pull up unreliable sources and flounder. When we assign a traditional resource paper, we often find to our dismay that the students complete it in a desultory manner, often plagiarizing and submitting lifeless information. But the WebQuest draws in a precise field and transforms what would otherwise be a dull task into an information adventure.

You will soon find that WebQuesting is a whole world. Right now, you can locate WebQuests on any topic you can think of and be ready to go. Or you can compose your own, alter an existing WQ, or even assign students to create their own WQs. In fact, ThinkQuest is an ongoing contest for student-created WQs.

WQs have become an educational genre. As such, they have structural features.

INTRODUCTION

The introduction is an invitation to the WQ. It should have an upbeat, invitational tone that speaks to the student in the second person. The introduction is best when it sets up an interesting scenario and is about 100 words long. Here are some ways to begin the introduction:

- Imagine that . . .
- You are a . . .
- Put yourself in the shoes of a . . .
- Once upon a time, . . .
- Have you ever thought about . . .
- Your telephone rings. It's . . .
- _____ needs your help.
- You are an expert in . . .
- Memorandum: _____

THE TASK

Also called *The Quest*, the task sets forth the objective of the investigation. The language of the task should be simple and direct. Many educators include learning objectives in the task. In a sense, the task is a rubric. Like a rubric, it delineates features that the finished product should have. Be sure that this section of the WQ is visually clear. Use a numbered or bulleted list.

PROCESSES AND RESOURCES

This is where you insert your Hotlist for the WQ. The Hotlist is a collection of Internet resources that you require or suggest. You may include directions for the students to locate additional resources on their own. You can easily learn how to set up Hotlists through a free service called Filamentality (www.filamentality.com) or a subscriber service called Web-n-Flow (www.webnflow.com).

CONCLUSION

The conclusion poses higher level questions that the students should now be able to address. Remember that WebQuesting is not about compiling facts that could be copied from a single source. WebQuesting is about problem-solving, pursuing information in search of enlightenment, examining multiple points of view.

The conclusion redirects students to the learning objectives set forth in the Task.

SUMMARY

When we say "research paper," what exactly do we mean? Students need clear expectations *from each department*. If we want students to do research, that is, to go beyond themselves for information and understandings, we can be imaginative as well as traditional. WebQuests are imaginative scenarios in which students use the Internet to solve problems. But as we teach research papers, we need to do just that, offering models, explicit instruction, and skill-building activities.

8

NOTEBOOKS AND JOURNALS
I WRITE, THEREFORE I THINK . . .

CHAPTER OVERVIEW

The relationship between writing and thinking is inextricable. In all subject areas, teachers need to know how to use notebook and journal writing to exploit this connection.

This chapter answers these questions:

- ♦ How can I assess notebooks and journals?
- ♦ What are some effective and engaging journal prompts in my subject area?
- ♦ How can journal writing connect my subject to other subjects, to strengthen learning across the board?
- ♦ What are some novel ideas that will spark interdisciplinary thinking?

When we think of notebooks, we usually picture students copying from a chalkboard or scrambling to grab words from the air as the teacher lectures at the podium. But a notebook can do more than record teacher-directed information. Properly directed, a notebook can be a *means of thinking*, a way for the learner to connect one class to another, an interdisciplinary journal.

THE ACROSS-THE-BOARD JOURNAL

Imagine Jessica. She's a ninth grade student whose teachers actually speak to each other. These teachers know that in English this month, Jessica is reading Greek mythology; in social studies, she's studying the Middle Ages; in earth science, she's learning about weather patterns; and in math, she's doing properties of triangles. Jessica's teachers are mindful that Jessica's day does not begin and end with their class. They ask her to make connections.

Jessica has a notebook that she refers to as her Ninth Grade Journal. She carries it from class to class, because a few times a week, in each class, Jessica uses her Across-the-Board Journal.

RULES OF ENGAGEMENT

♦ The left side page of a book or a notebook is called the verso. The right side page is called the recto. You will write your drafts on the verso, your revisions on the recto. Your teachers won't read the verso unless you indicate on the recto that you did not need to rewrite. Writings on all pages to be read by the teacher (that is, all recto pages) are to be neatly presented and correctly spelled.

♦ Each entry should consist of two or three well-developed sentences.

♦ You will hand your notebook in every two weeks to your _____ teacher. It will be evaluated according to the rubric.

LOGISTICS: Q & A

♦ Q: How are the journals graded? Who grades what? What are the standards? What about spelling, punctuation, and so on? How often is the journal handed in?

Teachers divide the grading of the journals among themselves. One way to decide who gets what is simply to divide the students alphabetically. A two-week interval works well, with the assumption that the journals will be returned after one week, thus giving the journals a rest for one week. The journals are evaluated against a rubric, which accounts for correctness and presentation.

♦ Q: Doesn't this create excessive paperwork?

Assuming that the student will be doing journal entries once or twice per week, that each entry has two or three sentences, and that the journal is being kept in four classes, the teacher would read anywhere from 16 to 48 sentences. Remember that each teacher would be collecting only one-fourth of the total number of journals.

RUBRIC: ACROSS THE BOARD JOURNAL (RATE EACH CATEGORY 1-5)

Language Tone: The student has used proper terminology, rather than casual, imprecise language.

1	2	3	4	5

Completeness: The student has written two or three well-developed sentences and has responded to prompts for each class.

1	2	3	4	5

Presentation: The student's presentation is legible and follows the conventions of standard written English: spelling, punctuation, sentence structure, and capitalization.

1	2	3	4	5

Content: The student's expression is clear and sensible, showing insight, depth, and thought.

1	2	3	4	5

Scoring: Add each category. Multiply by 5.

JOURNAL PROMPTS

The journal prompts come in two flavors. Structural prompts can be used for any class, regardless of content. These are prompts such as *wrap-ups, key terms, questions, I think of,* and *three action words.* Thematic prompts are a little more difficult to apply across the board. Some of these prompts, such as relating the subject to a particular quotation, may not fit all subjects on a given day. The teacher whose subject matter for a given two-week period is not applicable to a thematic topic may opt to give another topic or just take a pass. It should be said, though, that sometimes, students can make connections that their teachers may have overlooked.

Keep in mind that journal writing is a less formal mode of expression than essay writing. Although we do insist upon rewrites and correct spelling, we do not necessarily require complete sentences. We make a distinction between *sentence form* and *notation form.* Notation form can include phrases, quick definitions, lists, labeled diagrams, and fragments.

As a writing-to-think activity, the journal does not require the stringent requirements of the formal essay. The journal functions as a "thought lab" in which the writer needs latitude, some freedom from the tight organizational structure of the formal essay. However, just to develop constructive habits of mind, we do expect legibility and correct spelling, especially of technical terms.

STRUCTURAL PROMPTS (APPLICABLE TO ALL SUBJECTS)

WRAP-UPS

Summarize the main points of today's lesson: If an absentee asked you what we did today, what would you say? (*sentence form*)

♦ English

In Act III, Scene II of R & J, Juliet says, "O serpent heart, hid with a flow'ring face." She means that a handsome face can hide an evil heart. She thinks Romeo was evil to have slain her cousin Tybalt. This speech is made up of opposites to express how she feels deceived by Romeo's appearance.

♦ Biology: A Punnett Square shows the different combinations of dominant and recessive alleles:

	T	t
t	Tt	
t	Tt	

♦ Social Studies: *The Industrial Revolution was a turning point in civilization. It began in England (Liverpool, Manchester, London). It is symbolized by the steam-powered engine. Iron and coal were the main ingredients of the I.R.*

♦ Math: *An equation is a mathematical sentence. It has two expressions that are separated by an equals sign. The value of a variable can depend on the value of another variable: 21x.*

KEY TERM

Write two or three technical terms that apply to this subject, and give examples or associations. (*Note:* the terms don't have to be new. They just have to be terms that would be in a glossary for this subject.) (*Notation form*)

♦ English

<u>Juxtaposition</u>: *the placement of two opposites near each other so that we see the contrast:"Was ever book containing such vile matter so fairly bound?"*

<u>Iambic pentameter</u>: *ten syllables, accent on every second syllable:"Did ever dragon keep so fair a cave?"*

♦ Biology

<u>Alleles</u>: *two genes associated with a particular characteristic, such as green eyes*

<u>Homozygous pair</u>: *an allelic pair of the same genes, such as two dominants or two recessives*

♦ Social Studies

<u>Urbanization</u>: *the influx of people into cities because of changes in society. Associated with slums, overcrowding, disease, high out-of-wedlock pregnancy rates, prostitution*

<u>Proletariat</u>: *Karl Marx's term for the working class; people who produce goods but do not own the factories; associated with the Communist Manifesto (1848)*

♦ Math

<u>Dependent variable</u>: *Y is the dependent variable when its value depends upon the value of X; graphed on vertical axis*

<u>Independent variable</u>: *X is the independent variable when the value of Y is dependent upon it; graphed on the horizontal axis*

BEFORE/AFTER

Write a before/after statement relevant to the current topic.

- English: *Juliet trusts Romeo before he slays her cousin Tybalt. After that, she mistrusts him.*

- Biology: *Before fertilization, homologous chromosomes separate and move in a way known as random segregation. After fertilization, alleles recombine to produce new gene combinations.*

- Social Studies: *Before reformers enacted laws that improved working conditions, there was widespread misery caused by overcrowding, disease, pollution, and industrial accidents. After unions were established, conditions for workers improved.*

- Math: *R equals the number of rectangles and P equals the perimeter of the figure. Before we can figure out the equation, we need to know the total length of the left and right sides of the rectangles. After that, we can write an expression that represents the perimeter.*

TYING THE THREADS

At this point in her journal, having responded to three prompts, Jessica will consider how what she's learning in these four classes ties together. She is asked to find similar themes and details in what she's learning. What patterns appear? What assumptions carry through the day?

> *As I look over my last three journal topics, I notice that a lot has to do with two's. Romeo and Juliet are two lovers who come from two warring families. Juliet realizes that she has two feelings for Romeo: love and anger. She sees two sides of him and of her own feelings.*
>
> *Alleles are pairs of traits. They can be two of the same (homologous) or one of each (dominant and recessive).*
>
> *The Industrial Revolution had both good and bad. It was bad because of the terrible misery of the workers. It was good because it brought more jobs and wages after the reformers improved conditions. It brought us to the modern age. Technology brings both good and bad.*
>
> *In math we did equations. Equations are a sentence with two sides. We plot the dependent variable on the vertical axis and the independent variable on the horizontal axis.*

The level of Jessica's writing here is probably not the best she could do if she were to buff and polish the piece with more examples, connectors, vocabulary elevation, and other techniques of serious writing. As a tie-up activity, Jessica's casual writing serves to reinforce her learning and to unify her school day.

ENGLISH/
BIOLOGY

SOCIAL
STUDIES/
MATH

INTERDIS-
CIPLINARY

TRIANGULATION

Consider how the issues you are learning about form three points, like a triangle or a lever.

- ◆ English: *Romeo and Juliet and Friar Lawrence form a triangle: Friar Lawrence is trying to help them, but this is an ironic triangle because FL is actually the agent of their deaths by his actions.*

- ◆ Biology: *Genetics forms a triangle because you have the two parents and the offspring. The offspring is made up of the parents but is its own unique organism.*

- ◆ Social Studies: *The Industrial Revolution forms a triangle between the rural areas, the cities, and the people. The people migrated to the cities in huge numbers, which changed everything in the rural areas and the cities.*

- ◆ Math: *An equation is a triangle. It has two expressions and an equal sign. The equal sign acts as a fulcrum on a seesaw that is balanced.*

I THINK OF . . .

What does this issue remind you of? Connect this issue to something else you've learned about in school, or to a movie or story, or to a situation or object in your life. Stay away from the obvious. Try to think of a connection that no one else in the class will have. *Note:* The *I think of. . .* statement is not asking for your opinion. It is asking you to be *reminded* of something.

- ◆ English: *When I think of how Friar Lawrence is the agent of death when he's supposedly the agent of love, I think of how you can die from taking too much of certain medicines, which are supposed to help you get better.*

INTERDIS-
CIPLINARY

- ◆ Biology: *I think of how two primary colors make a new color which looks like both colors but is also its own unique color. Red and yellow = green.*

- ◆ Social Studies: *I think of sweatshops today in Asia where people (some children) work for poor wages to make goods that Americans buy at the mall. But plenty of Americans have lost their jobs when companies go overseas to hire cheap labor.*

- ◆ Math: *I think of a mobile and how any change makes it go lopsided.*

CURRENT ISSUES

How does what you are learning this week connect to a controversial issue in our society?

INTERCIS-
CIPLINARY

- ◆ English: *Teenage sex, secrecy from parents, drugs, gangs, kids who rebel against their parents.*

- ◆ Biology: *A major controversy of today is cloning, which is based on understanding genetics.*

- Social Studies: *In our society, we have the computer revolution, which has changed how people live and work and communicate.*

- Math: *You could make an equation that shows the relationship between the stock market, and employment, and inflation rates today.*

TYING THE THREADS

When I look back at my journal writings, I think about connections and relationships and how everything effects everything else. Everything is like an equation but sometimes, like in Romeo and Juliet with Friar Lawrence giving Juliet the death potion you don't know how things are affecting the equation. All of these subjects are about ways to solve problems to make things better but sometimes the solutions make things worse. Then sometimes it gets better again but you have to pay a price.

INTERDISCIPLINARY LANGUAGE

The next four journal prompts ask the students to use the terminology of one subject to describe what they are learning in another.

LITERARY TERMS

Use literary terms, such as *irony*, to discuss what you've learned in biology, social studies, and math.

- English/Biology: *Like a word that is out of <u>rhyme</u>, mutations interfere with genetic <u>rhythm</u> and expectations.*

- English/Social Studies: *In both the Russian and French revolutions, bread was the <u>metaphor</u> for widespread frustration at the excesses of the ruling classes who refused to respond to the needs of the masses.*

- English/Math: *A matrix is <u>like a poem</u> because the numbers in the matrix, <u>like the words in the poem</u> are not interchangeable. In a poem, each word must have a certain meaning, sound, and number of syllables.*

BIOLOGICAL TERMS

Use biological terms to discuss what you've learned in English, social studies, and math.

- Biology/English: *By crossing the lines of the feud between the Capulets and the Montagues, R & J disrupted the <u>ecosystem</u> of Gerona, igniting murderous warfare.*

- Biology/Social Studies: *The model of the Bolshevik revolution of 1917 <u>replicated itself</u> in other revolutions, such as China and Cuba.*

- Biology/Math: *If organisms within the same ecosystem have a positive association, then factors that affect the ecosystem affect these organisms similarly.*

SOCIAL STUDIES TERMS

Use social studies terms to discuss what you've learned in English, biology, and math.

- Social Studies/English: *Gerona was the scene of <u>guerrilla warfare</u>, with one bloody scene after another, ending with an ironic <u>cease-fire</u>.*

- Social Studies/Biology: *Cancer cells <u>colonize</u> neighboring organs, <u>enslaving</u> their cells.*

MATHEMATICAL TERMS

Use mathematical terms to discuss what you've learned in English, social studies, and biology.

- Math/English: *Violence increased <u>exponentially</u>, as each murder led to vengeance.*

- Math/Social Studies: *The brutality of the Bolsheviks proved <u>equal to</u> that of the czar, and the reality of worldwide socialism proved <u>inversely proportionate to</u> its idealism.*

- Math/Social Studies: *Trotsky established a brutal military <u>equation</u> in forming his Workers' and Peasants' Red Army. On one side were the Bolsheviks. They kept watch (threatened) over the loyalty of the other side, which consisted of some former czarist officers, who were there because of their experience which the new army needed.*

- Math/Biology: *Cell division <u>multiplies</u> cells in a <u>geometric progression</u>.*

TYING THE THREADS

This was hard. I had to think about two meanings at once. I did the math statements by looking in the glossary of my math text, but a lot of the words seemed like they could be used for anything, not just math. I always thought math was just about numbers. Math is about numbers but it's also about how different parts of a problem are related and similar .It was easiest to do biology and math. The social studies words were mostly about wars and aggression. The English words were hard to think of for other subjects.

OTHER STRUCTURAL PROMPTS

- Flow Charts, which express the subject matter in terms of the breakdown of its parts and use arrows to show relationships.
- Cause/effect statements
- Contrasts
- Pattern-finding
- Geometric forms

THEMATIC PROMPTS

QUOTATIONS

The next two journal entries ask the student to view the themes and information in each class through the lens of quotations.

FIRST QUOTATION

Things fall apart. The center cannot hold.
Mere anarchy is loosed upon the world,
The blood-dimmed tide is loosed, and everywhere
The ceremony of innocence drowned;
The best lack all conviction, while the worst
Are full of passionate intensity.
(from "The Second Coming" by William Butler Yeats)

♦ English: *In R & J things fall apart and anarchy is loosed upon the world when Tybalt slays Mercutio. When Romeo avenges Mercutio's death by slaying Tybalt, the Prince banishes Romeo and he ends up not getting Friar Lawrence's message about Juliet not being really dead. "The best" could be seen as love, while "the worst" could be seen as violence and revenge.*

♦ Biology: *This quote reminds me of what could happen in an ecosystem which is overhunted or overfished. The "center" is the natural balance that holds an ecosystem together.*

♦ Social Studies: *This quote makes me think about everything we've ever learned in history. Systems change and collapse and become new systems which are usually pretty much like the old. Lenin and the Red Army were just as oppressive as the czars.*

♦ Math: *When we make any change to one side of an equation without counterbalancing on the other side, things fall apart. The center cannot hold. But math isn't a matter of the best and the worst. Math is the opposite of anarchy. Math is the ultimate control.*

SECOND QUOTATION

We are in the presence of a disaster of the first magnitude.
(Winston Churchill's response to the Munich Agreement, 1938)

♦ English: *The death of Romeo and Juliet is a disaster of the first magnitude. Disaster means "under a bad star". R & J are "star-crossed lovers".*

♦ Biology: *In biology, a disaster of the first magnitude occurs when cell division goes out of control, as in cancer.*

♦ Social Studies: *Winston Churchill was referring to the disaster of the first magnitude that happened after Neville Chamberlain agreed to allow Hitler to invade Czechoslovakia (the Sudetenland).*

OTHER QUOTATIONS (FROM SHAKESPEARE)

Now does he feel his robes hang loose about him like a giant's robe upon a dwarfish thief. (*Macbeth*)

Thus may we gather honey from the weed,
And make a moral of the devil himself. (*Henry V*)

So shall you hear
Of carnal, bloody, and unnatural acts,
Of accidental judgments, casual slaughters,
Of deaths put on by conning and (forced) cause,
And, in this upshot, purposes mistook
Fallen on the inventors' heads. (*Hamlet*)

OTHER THEMATIC PROMPTS

- ♦ Problem-solvers: Pose a problem to which today's lesson is a solution.
- ♦ Newspaper connections: What items on the front page of today's newspaper connect to what we are learning this week?
- ♦ Draw a Venn diagram that compares the topic under study to a similar topic.

100 TOOLBOX WORDS

The idea behind the 100 Toolbox Words strategy is to make connections with clear, concise language. Jessica refers to this list frequently in all classes, looking for ways to express what she knows. Because these are strong, basic, all-purpose words, Jessica finds that she can process information into her own words.

Jessica's first challenge is to match a particular toolbox word to the concept at hand. Then Jessica writes an accurate, concise sentence, but she has to be careful not to abandon the technical terminology altogether. The goal of academic writing is to balance lay terminology, such as the words on the toolbox list, with the specialized language in the domain of the subject.

Lewis Thomas, author of *The Lives of a Cell*, *Medusa and the Snail*, and various other books about science, was a master at expressing technical concepts with the right balance of lay and specialized terminology. In the following paragraph, from *The Lives of a Cell*, Thomas speaks about the applications of scientific research:

> We have to face, in whatever discomfort, the real possibility that the level of insight into the mechanisms of today's unsolved diseases—schizophrenia, for instance, or cancer, or stroke—is comparable to the situation for infectious disease in 1875, with similarly crucial bits of information still unencountered. We could be that far away, in the work to be done if not in the years to be lived through.

If this is the prospect, or anything like this, all ideas about better ways to speed things up should be given open-minded, close scrutiny.

Long-range planning and organization on a national scale are obviously essential. There is nothing unfamiliar about this; indeed, we've been engaged in a coordinated national effort for over two decades, through the established processes of the National Institutes of Health. Today's question is whether the plans are sharply focused enough, the organization sufficiently tight. Do we need a new system of research management, with all the targets in clear display, arranged to be aimed at?

This would seem reassuring and tidy, and there are some important disease problems for which it has already been done effectively, demonstrating that the direct, frontal approach does work. Poliomyelitis is the most spectacular example. Once it had been learned (from basic research) that there were three antigenic types of virus and that they could be abundantly grown in tissue culture, it became a certainty that a vaccine could be made. Not to say that the job would be easy, or in need of any less rigor and sophistication than the previous research; simply that it could be done. Given the assumption that experiments would be carried out with technical perfection, the vaccine was a sure thing. It was elegant demonstration of how to organize applied science, and for this reason it would have been a surprise if it had not succeeded.

("The Planning of Science" from *The Lives of a Cell*, pp. 118-19, by Thomas, Lewis Thomas. Copyright ©1974 by Lewis Thomas; Copyright ©1971 by the Massachusetts Medical Society. Used by permission of Viking Penguin, a division of Penguin Putnam, Inc.)

Thomas's writing is accessible and interesting because he intersperses specialized language with the vernacular. The trick is to establish a balance of word types. So Jessica looks at her list of toolbox words and sees how she can fit them in with the specialized terms that she's learned in biology.

- ◆ Sounds natural: *Glaciers pick up and transport particles of various sizes. The particles have life forms and nutrition for life forms sticking to them. This shows how glacial movement patterns affect the ecosystem.*

- ◆ Sounds contrived and wordy: *The rock layers in a plateau are horizontal in the way they are slanted.*

THE TOOLBOX WORD LIST

ashes	crawl	gem	pick	shout	strong
balloon	crumble	glass	piece	shower	swirl
black	dark	grab	plant	shrink	switch
bond	deep	grip	point	sink	teeth
break	door	hammer	press	slant	thread
bring	doubt	harm	raise	sleep	throw
brush	drain	harsh	range	slip	tie
bubble	eye	heat	river	soften	touch
build	face	jet	route	splash	tough
burst	fall	jump	scrape	splinter	tug
cap	flash	jungle	scramble	split	tumble
cash	float	key	shadow	squeeze	twist
catch	flow	light	shallow	stand	weak
close	flower	line	sheet	step	weave
color	fly	link	shift	storm	work
cover	forest	mix	shoot	strike	wrong
crash	game	night	shorten		

This list may seem random, but all of these words are Anglo/Saxon, which means that they've come to the English language from Germanic tribes. Anglo/Saxon words, with their clear meanings and strong sounds, form the basis of the English language. These are words that have come into Jessica's vocabulary without effort. She's comfortable and sure about them.

But since the list is arbitrary, Jessica is free to add and replace as her journal develops. It's easy to recognize an Anglo/Saxon word (or, as we prefer to say, a "toolbox word") by the following characteristics:

ADDING TO THE TOOLBOX

♦ Words of one or two syllables

♦ Often have a consonant blend at the beginning or end of the word, or both

♦ Often have the *gh* or *ght* combination

♦ Often have a silent *e*

100 BRIEFCASE WORDS

Serviceable and sturdy as the toolbox words are, Jessica needs a few words that sound more educated. In addition to the specialized language that would appear in the glossary of a textbook, there are Latinate or Greek-based words, the kind that appear in a vocabulary list for English class. We call these the *briefcase words* because they have a lawyerly, formal style. Jessica is a little intimidated by some of these words, a bit uncomfortable, because she doesn't use them much in her speech. But she does know that Latinate or Greek-based words belong in academic writing and that her teachers seem more at ease with them than she does.

The briefcase words have an elevated, educated sound because they all have a Latin or Greek root. Latinate and Greek-based words have a certain air about them. They sound smart, but, if we overuse them, they sound stuffy. Sentences that overuse Latinate words begin to lose their human touch, as in the sentences below:

♦ Sounds natural: *The theory of punctuated equilibrium states that species stay the same for long periods of time (millions of years). At various points in those millions of years, intense geological changes burst in. That is when new species may develop.*

♦ Too many Latin/Greek based words: *The hypothesis of punctuated equilibrium posits that species stabilize for extended time periods which could encompass millions of years. These periods of extended stability can be sporadically interrupted by episodic geologic developments during which new species can evolve.*

20 ROOTS FOR BRIEFCASE WORDS

Root: ag, act, ig (drive, urge)

agent	coagulate	agitate	agile	counteract

Root: alt (high)

altitude	altar	exalt	altimeter	alto (formerly, high male voice)

Root: aster (star)

asteroid	astronomy	asterisk	aster	disaster

Root: aur (gold)

aura	aurora	ornate	oriole	gaudy

Root: cad, cas, cid (fall)

cadence	occasion	accident	casualty	deciduous

Root: ced, cess (go, yield)

accede, accession	concede, concession	precede, precedent	intercede, intercession	secede, secession

Root: cogit (know)

recognize	cogitate	cognate	precognition	incognito

Root: commun (common)

community	Communism	communal	communicate	communion

Root: contra (oppose)

contradict	contrapositive	contraband	contrary	contrast

Root: corpus (body)

| corpse | corpuscle | incorporate | corpulent | corporation |

Root: cosm (order)

| cosmic | cosmopolitan | microcosm | macrocosm | cosmetic |

Root: cresc, cret (grow)

| crescent | accrete, accretion | discrete, discretion | excrete, excretion | secrete, secretion |

Root: curr, curs (run)

| current | cursor | course | discourse | recourse |

Root: sequ, secu (follow)

| sequence | consequent | subsequent | prosecute | consecutive |

Root: simil (like)

| simulate | assimilate | simultaneous | similitude | similar |

Root: sist (stand)

| persist | resist | subsist | consist | insist |

Root: tag, tang, tig (touch)

| contagion | tangent | intangible | contiguous | contingent |

Root: tend, tent (stretch)

| extend | tension | tendon | contend | tender |

Root: tort (twist)

| torture | extort | distort | contort | tortuous |

Root: turb (confuse, drive)

| turbulent | turbine | disturb | turbid |

As a tenth grade student, Jessica knows most of these words, but the list reminds her to use them. In her English class, most of the words on her vocabulary lists have Latin/Greek roots, as will the words that she meets on her SATs and other standardized tests for college entrance. Jessica understands that her language is like her wardrobe in that different levels of formality are expected according to the occasion: her writing vocabulary is more formal than her everyday speaking vocabulary.

OTHER JOURNAL PROMPTS

♦ Problem-Solving: Is there a problem for which what we are learning this week is the solution or could lead to a solution?

Biology: *This week we learned the categories of organic compounds found in living things. These are carbohydrates, lipids, proteins, and nucleic acids. This information can solve the problem of understanding what the basis of life is all about and how the "chemical factory" of the cell is supposed to work. Understanding this can help scientists fix things that go wrong or out of balance in the cells.*

♦ Lists: What lists can be generated by what we are learning this week? For our purposes, there are four types of lists:

  • Classification: Shows categories and subcategories

Biochemistry

Inorganic Compounds	*Organic Compounds*	
water	carbohydrates:	sugars
salts		starches
acids/bases	lipids:	fats
		oils
		waxes
	proteins:	functional
		structural
	nucleic acids:	dna
		rna

  • Etymology: Shows word families

  Carbohydrates: carbon, bicarbonate, carbonated, carbon dating, carbon cycle

  Hydrogen, hydrophobia, hydrant, hydrolysis

  • Examples: Shows specifics

  Types of mutagens

  Radiation: x-rays, ultraviolet, radioactive substances, cosmic rays

  Chemicals: formaldehyde, benzene, PCBs, asbestos

  • Spreadsheet: shows comparative characteristics:

Flora	Fauna	Climate	Examples
Deserts			
Rain forests			
Tundra			
Plains			

♦ Popular Culture: Is there an issue in the news which refers to what we've learned this week?

This week there was a case where two babies were switched at birth and given to the wrong parents. The mother found out by DNA testing that the child she thought was hers was not the child that she had given birth to.

OTHER JOURNAL APPLICATIONS

WRITING YOUR WAY INTO KNOWING

Jessica uses her math journal to "think her way through" her math problems:

> *The probability that an event will occur is 4/9. I have to figure out the probability that the event will not occur. I have to subtract 1 from the probability that the event will occur (4/9). 1 subtracted from 4/9: I add 1 plus 4 and use the same denominator. Equals 5/9 that the event will not occur. If it's a little less than half that it will not occur, then it's a little more than half that it will occur.*

If Jessica's mode of learning is verbal, rather than symbolic, then she can puzzle out the math problem by taking it through in words rather than in symbols. In her last sentence, she sees whether her solution makes logical sense to her when she expresses the conditions in terms that make sense to her.

Many students work through math problems by talking out loud as they work. We often observe people doing this as they sift through the work piled on their desks. They talk their way into knowing. We often talk our way into knowing in the course of social conversations in which we thank a friend for helping us come to a solution that we came to all by ourselves, just by talking it through.

Writing can work this way: we can use writing to "talk ourselves through" a puzzle, such as a math problem, or through an organizational quagmire, such as how to file complicated insurance or how to go about writing a research report.

REFLECTION/METACOGNITION/THINKING ABOUT THINKING

As learners, we operate on two planes. One plane is processing the information itself for its own sake, but the other plane has to do with stepping back and looking at our own style of learning. The following questions help Jessica to assess her learning:

- How did I learn what I've learned this week? *took a lot of notes; studied with Michele for quiz; did the lab; drew diagram*
- What am I unsure of? *don't understand how to do the last column of the truth table; don't get how to set up the truth table with information given*
- What am I sure of? *know how to do the truth tables with just the and/or signs; know how to fill in table if table is already set up*
- How can I use what I've learned to learn something else? *can figure out conjunctions (and) and disjunctions (or); can use this to figure out if p represents "x is a prime number" and q represents "x is an even number greater than 2" that one of the given statements is true (question 3)*

JOURNAL WRITING FOR IN-CLASS RESPONSE

Journals can be useful in helping students organize their thoughts before giving an oral response. Jessica is not one of those students whose hand pops up to answer questions even though she has good ideas and questions to contribute. She's a little nervous about finding the right words and would just as soon leave it to her classmates to keep the momentum going.

But Jessica's social studies teacher gives everyone time to jot down ideas before being asked to speak. This *think time* works well not only because it gives Jessica more confidence to speak, but also because her notes remain in her journal for reference. Jessica's social studies teacher, Mrs. Riley, doesn't ask questions like "What is the capital of Bulgaria?" Her question, and Jessica's journal responses, are more like this:

- How is the Balkan conflict similar to the Arab/Israeli conflict? *ethnic fighting; different religious groups; once was unified by imperialist power (USSR/Britain); powder keg for extended fighting*

- How is poverty related to disease? *can't afford medicine; have to work, overcrowding, not enough doctors in poor areas, can't work because sick*

- How is famine related to war? *enemies withhold food, cut off food supplies, block transportation of food*

SUMMARY

The across-the-board journal is a vehicle for informal writing in which the student processes and connects information, language, and problem-solving skills from one class to another. It is not meant to replace the traditional content area notebook. In order for the across-the-board journal to work, the following conditions need to be in place:

- **Communication**

  At least *two* teachers need to agree on the contents and requirements of the journal. What are students expected to do? What are teachers expected to do?

- **Writing Standards**

  Although the journal represents informal writing, at some point the student needs to rewrite *parts* of it. The teacher evaluating the journal is entitled to read something that is neat, legible, and correct.

- **Comfort Level**

  If the students (and the teachers) don't view the journal as a means for helping them to learn, rather than for making them miserable, then the journal fails in its purpose.

♦ A Clear and Simple System

Because several teachers are involved, the journal has to function under a system which is easy and natural for both students and teachers to live with. If the directions are too complicated, if what goes where is more important than what gets written, then the project will fall of its own weight.

♦ Small Pieces

If the journal entries are too long, the task of reading them will overwhelm most teachers and the project will be discontinued. Practicality is paramount.

SUGGESTIONS

♦ Start Small

Plan on doing the journal for short periods of time, such as a quarter of the year.

♦ Use Class Time to Write

Students tend to take writing more seriously if they are writing under the direct guidance and modeling of the teacher. Assigning journal entries for homework is likely to lead to careless presentation, copying, and neglect. Ten or fifteen minutes weekly should prove a valuable use of class time. Rewrites can be done at home.

♦ Show Exemplars

Let students see model journals.

♦ Learn Outside Your Field

The across-the-board journal is a splendid opportunity for teachers to learn what the student's whole day is like and where their classes fits in. Learning about other classes makes our own classes more interesting, not only to the students, but to us. We model lifelong learning habits to our students when we refer to other content areas in our classes.

9

NOTE-TAKING
FOR FUTURE REFERENCE

CHAPTER OVERVIEW

Note-taking is a part of every class, but it often amounts to mere copying of predigested notes off the board. This chapter presents various models of note-taking that engage the student in listening, discerning what's most important, and recording information in an independent, meaningful fashion. This chapter answers the following questions:

- ♦ How can I help students to manage their paperwork?
- ♦ How can I teach students to take notes from my lecture?
- ♦ How can I be a better lecturer?
- ♦ What are some organizational techniques and models for taking notes?

* * *

Bryant has had some trouble in general science this year. His test grades have been dismal, and he doesn't seem to know how to study. Tomorrow is the unit test on the grasshopper. One look at Bryant's notebook tells a story: It consists of mostly blank pages with lots of loose, folded papers stuck in. Bryant has answer sheets from a few old tests and quizzes, several study guides and random workbook pages, some diagrams and wordfind puzzles, a code for *Mortal Kombat*, a permission slip for a field trip to a military museum, a long-lost rough draft from an English composition, and some torn-out pages with various jottings, cross-outs, and reminders. If this notebook had four walls, a floor, and a ceiling, it would be Bryant's room.

Bryant needs a system, *and* he needs to learn how to take and use notes. The further along we go in education, the more we receive information through lecture. Therefore, middle schools and high schools would do well to acclimate students to the lecture format, to train them, over time, to listen, take notes, and then use their notes to reinforce and apply information. This chapter presents teaching strategies that help students to do the following:

- Work within a system of paper management.
- Take notes from a lecture.
- Take notes while doing research.
- Take notes from readings.
- Take notes to prepare in-class responses.

PAPER MANAGEMENT

The average anvil salesman carries a case of samples that weighs less than a ninth grader's backpack. Nevertheless, students need binders for each subject and various school supplies. A good paper management system consists of the following habits and materials:

- Go through your backpack every Friday. Discard or file all loose papers, wrappers, lunch remains, ticket stubs, newspapers, subpoenas, paper clips, and lint.
- Maintain a pocket folder to collect loose papers. Clear it every Friday.
- Use small binders instead of spiral notebooks. With a binder, you can save handouts, reorganize your notes, and add blank paper.
- Punch holes and use reinforcements on any papers that need to go into your binder. Papers that are forced into the rings without the benefit of hole-punching tend to jam the binder. Just as rolled up clothing stuffed into bureau drawers leads to the habit of draping clothing over chairs, when papers get jammed into the binder, we tend to resort to the crumple-and-stash-in-the-zippered-compartment-of-the-backpack method.

Most schools have time pockets such as homeroom and study hall. These would be ideal times for mass organization sessions in which all students would be expected to tend to their binders and lockers. A schoolwide policy that promotes productive work habits would include such rules and practices as

- No stuffing textbooks with papers.
- Accessibility to hole punchers and reinforcements.
- Time set aside for paper management.
- A well-stocked school store that offers packets of paper management supplies: small scissors, notebook-sized three-ring hole puncher, Scotch tape, pocket folder, reinforcements, liquid correction fluid, pens/pencils, ruler.
- The expectation that every student have a planner, with space for teacher/parent comments.
- Show models of exemplary notebooks, planners, schedules, work spaces.

Management of paper, time, and information is a life-long challenge, necessary for success in the workplace as well as the home. The teacher who helps Bryant organize his notebook does him immeasurable service, well worth the class time spent to do it.

NOTE-TAKING VS. COPYING

The teacher presents an outline and some labeled diagrams, and the students copy off the board. For many classes, this is called *taking notes*. Although there is value to this activity, in that it gets the student to attend and to see and copy words correctly spelled, there's more to the skill of note-taking than copying off the board. Verbatim copying does offer security to both teachers and students in that "everybody's getting everything." It is true that the process and discipline of copying has an inherent value so far as absorbing information is concerned. Nevertheless, Bryant has to actually learn various methods of shooting words down from the air and laying them out on paper. He has to learn shortcuts, setups, and styles.

TAKING NOTES FROM LECTURE

Note-taking from lecture is about three behaviors:
- The behavior of organization
- The behavior of concentration
- The behavior of listening

We've already talked about the behavior of organization. For Bryant to take proper notes, he needs to have his materials ready to go. His paper management system has to have brought him to the point where he has his notebook opened to the right page, dated for today's notes. Obvious as this is, Bryant is not in the habit of being open for business at the start of class. Rachel Billmeyer speaks of the effects of habits of mind on learning, regardless of skill or ability (Billmeyer, R. 1996. *Teaching Reading in the Content Areas: If Not Me, Then Who?* Aurora, CO: McCrel, p. 8.). Practicing the behavior of organization leads to what she refers to as the "productive mental disposition." To borrow from Shakespeare: "Some are born with a productive mental disposition, some achieve a productive mental disposition, some have a productive mental disposition thrust upon them." It is for the latter that we offer the following suggestions to the teacher:
- Greet students warmly as they enter the room. Make eye contact with students in all parts of the room.
- Rotate seating every ten weeks or so, so that "the kid in the back" gets to be "the kid in the front."
- Circulate around the room.

- Display a gentle sense of humor and a genuine interest in all students.
- Extinguish grudges.

Bryant's notes are best for classes in which he feels that the teacher cares about him and knows what he is up to. Where he is permitted to use his backpack as a desk pillow, excuse himself for frequent "breaks," hide his face under a baseball cap, gaze out the window like a landed aristocrat surveying his manor, he does just that. But where nothing less than a productive mental disposition is permitted, Bryant attends, takes notes, and even gets involved in the lesson.

Once Bryant is prepared and serious, he can practice the behavior of concentration and listening.

BEFORE THE LECTURE

Although it will represent a radical departure from his usual approach to the beginning of class, Bryant should anticipate the lecture by reviewing his notes from yesterday. Doing so will direct his mind towards today's material. Bryant is probably unsteady with yesterday's notes anyway, so, if he fails to review, he digs himself into a deeper hole of confusion as new information is added to a shaky foundation. But the habit of review before class serves a fundamental purpose other than the obvious: The habit of review ritualizes the learning experience, much as stretches and warm-up activities ritualize practice for sports games and daily practice. When we establish a pattern of *before, during, after*, we give the activity a wholeness that sets it apart from the casual and mundane.

DURING THE LECTURE

Writing is an aid to concentration and is one of the best ways that Bryant can force himself to listen. He often complains that he is bored in school, but his boredom is a result, not a cause of his uninvolvement. Bryant is learning the following techniques of concentration that will result in good note-taking:

- He listens for organizational cues: *This is important, there are three reasons, to summarize.*
- He has a system of abbreviations: *reasons, results, types of, causes.*
- He listens with his eyes as well as his ears. Bryant can tell by the teacher's body language what is important and what is a side trip. By giving his teacher the courtesy of looking at her, Bryant signals a willingness to learn.
- He refrains from contributing nonsequiturs such as *Is this on the test? Do we have to know this? I was absent. Did you correct our grasshopper test yet?*

Concentration, listening, and writing go together. In his charming little book on learning, *Study is Hard Work*, William Armstrong gives five suggestions for making oneself a better listener in a lecture hall (Armstrong, W. 1995. *Study Is Hard Work*. Boston: David R. Godine, p. 11):

- Don't sit in the back.
- Have empathy and respect for the speaker. Remember that she has spent a long time preparing for this lecture.
- Exhibit body language that shows concentration and respect for learning and for the speaker, in particular. Give the speaker your undivided attention.
- Hold questions until the end or until questions are asked for. The speaker may be about to answer your question in the course of the lecture.
- Have a little humility. Acknowledge that this lecturer can teach you something that you don't already know.

PARTING SHOTS

Bryant, like many of his classmates, can "smell the bell." But while he's packing up, his teacher is summarizing and announcing a change in a due date. She's hurriedly spewing out information that she knows is on the next quiz, but she's out-noised by the end-of-class hallway hum and early closeout.

AFTER THE LECTURE

Bryant should take a few minutes at home that evening to go over his lecture notes. He can highlight, clarify, peruse the corresponding chapter in the text, ask questions for the next day, and fill in facts and figures. If he's grounded and confined to a small space without human contact, he can even check his spelling of technical terms and make a concept map (a.k.a. graphic organizer, diagram, schematic). It is not entirely crazy to make note of other things that happened on the day of this lecture: the mind learns in clusters and associations. Sometimes, we recall what we've learned by bringing to mind what we were wearing when we learned it.

SKILLS OF THE LECTURER: STAND AND DELIVER

Current pedagogical trends steer the teacher away from lecturing and toward cooperative learning, project-oriented, performance-based assessments. Nevertheless, we all know that listening and note-taking skills are essential not only in schools (especially college level) but also in the workplace. Despite the current parlance of the teacher as "facilitator," veteran teachers know that no matter how much "facilitating" we do, a certain amount of lecturing will always be in the gig. Knowing how to deliver a good lecture is to the master teacher what making the perfect soufflé is to the master chef.

- **Lay it out.** The overview should consist of the main points of the lecture, as well as its key terminology. Write key terms on the board so that listeners can see how they are spelled and relate them to words that they already know. Present an outline or schema and refer to it.

- **Set ground rules.** Before going into details, reveal to students what they are expected to write down. Should they write down examples? names? dates? research sources? What topics will be developed in future units? What areas are covered in the text?

- **Work the room.** People in the back tend to disengage, which is often why they choose to sit in the back. Don't let anyone escape from you. Convey energy by moving around, getting different perspectives. Make eye contact. Personalize questions and comments. In the presence of a great classroom lecturer, every student feels noticed.

- **Do a props check.** In this business, you have to be your own stage manager. There's nothing like having to paw through a stack of overhead transparencies to break the spell of a lecture. Don't skimp on the time it takes to check readability, legibility, and correctness. You can be certain that your students will take delight in interrupting your train of thought to point out a misspelling.

- **Tell anecdotes.** Anecdotes establish visuals and metaphor. As long as the anecdote doesn't meander, it can be a powerful tool for getting listeners to engage and connect. Immature listeners tend to jump into anecdotes to insert that their Uncle Seymour did the same thing last Christmas, which reminds someone else of an episode of a sitcom. And thus does a good lecture deflate like a cheap pool raft.

- **Take the pause that refreshes.** Punctuate the lecture with process time. Give students a chance to catch up on their notes. Coach them as to what their notes should look like at this point. Have everyone hold their notebooks up. Encourage proper page usage: notes should sprawl and have plenty of white space for later additions.

- **Point in the right direction.** Use transitional words and refer to the overview and outline to let students know where they are in the course of the lecture. Remember that learning is a recursive process: you'll need to rewind and play back occasionally. .

- **Be animated.** Lecturing is an art. Trust your enthusiasm. Flaunt your passion for the subject.

- **Teach note-taking.** Show models, including your own notes. Check notebooks and give feedback.. Allow students to experiment with various formats. Be mindful that the lecture is an opportunity for students to learn how to learn.

♦ **Check pulses.** Break the lecture from time to time and ask questions that require application, reflection, paraphrase, further examples. Ask everyone to explain a key concept to a partner.

♦ **Empathize.** Unlike the reader, the listener cannot control the pace at which information is poured out. The lecturer knows more about the subject and is more fluent in it than the student. The student can easily go astray, dwelling on some concept or term that he only partially understands. Factor in the inevitable distractions of ambient noise and add the burden of having to keep up with written notes, and you can see why you need those "processing pauses."

♦ **Establish a *No-Slacker Zone*.** Everyone's behavior effects the learning atmosphere. Distractions can be overt, such as chattering and calling out, or covert, such as refusal to make eye contact or doing homework for another class during the lecture. It is the teacher's job to make each student feel part of the community of the class. Overlooking passive/aggressive behavior undermines the seriousness of purpose that a class must have, and its effect is to insult and diminish the offending student, sending him the message that it doesn't really matter if he's there or not. Moreover, when we fail to demand behavior that will be expected in the workplace and in social settings, we do students a grave disservice. The student whose head rests on his arms and who yawns in his teacher's face is likely to learn the lessons of courtesy the hard way.

TAKING NOTES WHILE DOING RESEARCH

TAKING NOTES ON INDEX CARDS

Index cards are the traditional medium for research notes because they are easily managed and rearranged. The notes and quotations can be written on one side, with the source information on the other. Note cards are available in different colors for easy grouping, and "5 × 8" cards are better than "3 × 5" cards.

Sticky flags and post-its are great for marking library books. Bryant might think he can remember what books have useful information for his report and where that information is located in them, but he needs notecards and post-its to keep track of what's where.

NOTECARD TIPS

♦ Remember to record the pages where particular quotes are found.

♦ Remember to write Q or use quotation marks around quotations.

♦ Keep notes short.

♦ Leave space on the cards.

♦ Don't number the cards, or use stick-on labels, which can be easily changed.

♦ Don't try to write the whole paper on the cards.

♦ Remember that note cards are supposed to be a help, not a hindrance or meaningless exercise, for writing the research paper. The cards should serve your needs.

TAKING NOTES FROM READING

Textbooks offer features such as headings, chapter overviews and summaries, boldface print, and other clues that aid comprehension and focus the reader on important points. The act of notetaking, even though the key features are already represented in the text, involves the reader in the task and reinforces his learning. All Bryant has to do to enhance his understanding of a text is to transform the chapter headings and subheadings into an outline.

When reading informational material that is not visually laid out as a textbook would be, Bryant can assume that each chapter will begin with an overview and close with a summary and that the first sentence of each paragraph will be the topic sentence. If he owns the text, he should make marginal notes and read with a highlighter in hand.

A good technique is to approach each chapter with questions: After reading the first paragraph of this chapter, what questions do I have?

Bryant should take up every opportunity he can to own books, such as review books and novels, that he can mark. As a novice highlighter, Bryant had to learn not to highlight everything. Now he has a system:

♦ Circle names and places.

♦ Underline numbers.

♦ Use an asterisk to mark themes.

♦ Write E in the margin for events.

♦ Write Q for passages containing information likely to appear on a quiz.

♦ Write W for passages likely to appear in an essay test.

All of this material is in the textbook.

WHY TAKE NOTES?

♦ Note-taking engages the errant mind. While taking notes, we are less likely to click on that mental screen-saver that sends our minds into sail-away mode.

♦ Note-taking uses up nervous energy that many of us have when we are sitting in a classroom or studying at home.

♦ The act of note-taking helps us remember, organize, and process information. Note-taking gives us ownership of information.

- Being a kinesthetic activity, note-taking is the learning mode of people who learn "through their hands."
- Writing generates knowing: Note-taking is the first step in the writing process

TROUBLE-SHOOTING FOR STUDENTS WHO TAKE TOO MANY OR TOO FEW NOTES

- **Prescription 1: Defining the Space**

Stephanie sets aside two pieces of paper for her notes on the chapter she is reading. She fills in the top of the first page and the bottom of the second page with notes on the beginning and end of her chapter, respectively. This way, she knows she has to fit all notes between what she's already written.

- **Prescription 2: Timing**

Cynthia tends to drift off, not taking enough notes as she listens to lectures. She times herself to take half a page of notes every ten minutes.

- **Prescription 3: Notes within Notes**

Jared takes everything down. He's learned to go home and highlight his own notes. This has cued him in to what's really important.

MODEL NOTES

Text/Lecture: The teacher (or text) says:

We've been talking about the lifestyle changes that the Industrial Revolution brought. Today, we're going to advance those ideas into the twentieth century. I'm going to give you an overview of the major figures of science and technology of the late/nineteenth and early twentieth centuries, as well as World War I and what happened after it, in the 1920s. I'm going to mention a lot of names that we'll hear more about later this week. Make sure you know what these people are associated with and what impact they had on the twentieth century.

The beginning of the twentieth century was marked by a technological and scientific revolution. Who were the major figures in science of the late nineteenth century? Alexander Graham Bell, Louis Pasteur and Thomas Edison. These men laid the groundwork for major technological developments of the twentieth century: the airplane, the automobile, the radio, the telephone, movies, central heating, electricity. Travel and communication were faster than ever before, so the world became smaller.

The irony of these advances is that although they made life easier for people who had the money to afford them, massive numbers of poor people were working in dangerous and back-breaking sweat-shops in cities. As cities grew, diseases that proliferate in over-crowded conditions thrived. Also, military weapons such as tanks and machine guns made war more deadly.

At the same time, scientific theories were altering man's perception of his place in the universe and what he could to change his environment. In the late nineteenth century an Austrian monk named Gregor Mendel discovered the nature of heredity. Marie and Pierre Curie discovered radioactivity. During the early part of the twentieth century, Albert Einstein came up with theories that would change how we think of space and time.

Another field of discovery and exploration was the field of human behavior. Ivan Pavlov and Sigmund Freud developed theories of human behavior that revolutionized the way people thought about their actions, their relationships, their motivations, their desires, and their self-control.

These radical developments were exciting and frightening at the same time. People were wondering if technology was a blessing or a curse, to be trusted or not. When one of the greatest technological wonders of all time, the Titanic, went down, that disaster symbolized the uneasy relationship between man and machine. The Wright brothers made their first flight at Kitty Hawk and later died in a plane crash. Henry Ford invented a new way of manufacturing: the assembly line. It was efficient, but the worker was no longer a craftsman, just one more machine part.

In spite of the problems that technology causes, people of the early twentieth century looked to technology as a cure-all. Then along came World War I in 1914. The war was stalemated. Technology brought mustard gas, nerve gas, trench warfare, machine guns. It was bloody beyond belief, useless, murderous of civilians, and brought a hollow victory to the Allies. It set the stage for the brutal totalitarian states of Hitler, Mussolini, Stalin, and Franco.

But the world became more interconnected and the confusion, bitterness, emptiness and pure misery that followed World War I gave rise to great heroism and great works of art. The Irish hero Eamon DeValera fought against, and lost to, the English forces in Ireland. Writers such as Isak Dinesen spoke out against the Nazis. Pablo Picasso painted Guernica, a stunning portrayal of the carnage of the Spanish Civil War.

Franz Kafka wrote *The Metamorphosis*, a weird story about a young man who wakes up one morning and finds that he is transformed into a cockroach. Irish poet William Butler Yeats wrote *The Second Coming*, a vision of an approaching monster that will be the antichrist (*World Masterpieces*. Upper Saddle River, New Jersey: Prentice Hall, 1996, pp. 1030-6).

FIVE MODELS FOR NOTE-TAKING

What follows are five model set-ups for taking various kinds of notes. Each set-up applies to a different mindset, a different way of viewing the material. Because note-taking, by definition, is quick and dirty, we can't worry about spelling, *but we do have to attend to spelling details at some point after the note-taking session is over.*

Now is not the time to save paper. Leave plenty of space for additions.

SET-UP I: KNOWN/NEW/NEXT

This note-taking format gets the student thinking about prior knowledge before hearing the lecture, and then invites a personal response. It's effective because it frames information in a learning context and then opens the door for further learning. One problem with it is the column structure. Many students find that they don't have enough room in the middle (main) column. A variation on the layout is simply to list the "Known," then draw a line under it, take notes from the lecture, draw another line, and then write the "Next" items. In any case, the three segments should be labeled. We could also use color-coding, rather than columns, to differentiate the three sections.

TEACHER INTRODUCTION

Hold your paper horizontally and divide it into three columns. Label the first column "Known," and jot down whatever you know about the early twentieth century. What images come to mind? What famous people do you know about? What inventions? Wars? Ideas? Don't write sentences; just make quick notes. Label the second column "New." In it, make notes on the lecture and readings. Write down categories, names, and events. Label the third column "Next" and jot down questions, elaborations, points of interest, as well other details that you realize you do know, although you didn't include them in the first column.

Known	New	Next
Statue of Liberty freedom of the slaves imgration	Inventors: Bell, Pastore, Edison Led to telephone, movies, electricity, radio, heating, better life worse life for workers-sweatshops, acidents, disease, teniments scientists: Mendle—heredy Curys-r-activity Einstein-time & space Behavure- Pablov, Froid Ford asembly line-worker is machine pple tht tchlgy cure; titanic problems w tchlgy War1 bloody bloody then, hitler, musoline, stalin, frank some heros some resist lots of books-man is cockroach	Why is Freud so famous? Was H Ford good or bad? Did both right brothers die? So that's why theres no airline named after them. What hapend in the Spanish Civil War? What does war painting look like? Model T

SET-UP II: THE BIG T

The Big T is used for comparisons, cause/effect, before/after, or any kind of polarity. It is more sophisticated than the Known/New/Next because the listener has to take in details and decide where they go on the schemata.

TEACHER INTRODUCTION

On your paper, draw a big T that takes up the whole page. Label the left side "positive" and the right side "negative." I'm going to read a passage (or, deliver a brief lecture) about changes in the late nineteenth/early twentieth century. As I read, write the names or events along the vertical line. Then, jot down notes about how these people or events are positive or negative. Some will be both.

Positive		Negative
improve comunications, transpt better life	inventions: radio, plane, heating	hard work in factory disease cities crowded
Ford- asmbly line understanding life, cells, mind, more jobs know more about phcs: time/space,Einstn	science: gentics Mendl r-– active-Curies phcs – Einstn Psych- Pavlov Froid	disasters: Titanic, Wright Bros die bloody, brutal, mustart gas, nerve gas, machine guns, asembly line
Allies Win, many deaths Art, lit, Picaso, Kafka, Dinesen,	WWI	Hitler, Stalin, Musolini, Franco aproching monster

SET-UP III: GUIDED REVIEW

This method builds in a way to reinforce learning by taking notes, then reducing them into key words, and then, later, recollecting the details using the key words as cues.

TEACHER'S INSTRUCTIONS

Divide your page into two columns. The left column should take up one third of the page. You will take in-class lecture notes on the right side column. After you hear the lecture and take your notes, you will write very brief summary notes based on your lecture notes. That is how you will review the material. Then, when you refer to your notes to study, you'll cover the right column and try to recall the details, using your summary notes.

Reduction (later)	Notes (now)
Late 19th/early 20th centuries: technological/scientific revolution inventions: transportation/ communication advantages/disadvantes names of inventors and scientists	Tech and sci revolution <u>Inventors of late 19th</u>: Bell, Pastore, Edison Led to telephone, movies, electricity, radio, heating, communic/ transport better life but worse life for workers-sweatshops, acidents, disease, teniments <u>scientists</u>: Austrian monk Mendle—heredy Curys-r-activity Einstein-time & space, modern pyhics Behavure- Pablov, Froid: why do we do things?
Industry: Ford	Ford asembly line-worker is machine good or bad pple tht tchlgy cure; titanic
Accidents	<u>problems</u> w tchlgy man and machine
WWI: new weapons	WarI 1914 brutality, mustard gas, nerve gas, machine guns trench warfare Allies won, but many deaths
Art and lit	then, hitler, musoline, stalin, frank some heros some resist
Rise of dictators in 1920s	Great lit and art: Picasso painting of Span Civ War Irish uprising vs Brits- Irish lose Amn dvlra leads lots of books-man is cockroach -Kafka

SET-UP IV: PHRASE/THEME

The phrase/theme method works best with material that has interesting language and imagery. The strength of this model is that it concentrates on powerful language. In a class that is dense with information, it's easy for students to overlook the big picture, the theme, in favor of the facts and figures. The phrase/theme method promotes elevated thinking. Students are left with a list of words that they can incorporate into their own language. It took Bryant a while, and many exemplars, to grasp the purpose of taking down the phrases. It never occurred to him that there were "phrases that he liked." He was used to picking off facts: names, dates, glossary terms. The shopping cart metaphor helped him to see that he was looking for phrases that didn't necessarily have to do with the facts of the case. Instead, he was looking for phrases that made the piece come alive.. Without these phrases, we could just as well have a list or a timeline.

TEACHER'S INSTRUCTIONS

Divide your paper into two equal parts. As I read the passage, you will jot down words and phrases that interest you and that you think are important to the message. Choose words and phrases that you would like to use yourself: just keep writing them down in rapid succession, but not so rapidly that you lose track of the meaning. Consider yourself on a shopping trip. You are pulling words off the shelves and putting them into your shopping basket. Then, after you've heard the passage and composed your list in the right hand column, you will write down the themes that apply to these words. Don't worry about specific facts and figures. This method of note-taking is not about detail. It's about language and themes. So, for now, don't worry so much about who did what, when. Just collect phrases that appeal to you.

Themes (later)	Shopping Cart of Words (Now)
technology and science were both good and bad	the world became smaller
	overcrowded conditions
	war more deadly
WWI was the worst war so far and what	man's perception of his place in the universe
happened next was even worse	think of space and time
	field of discovery
great art and heroism can come from	human behavior
terrible suffering	exciting and frightening
	blessing or a curse
whenever we solve a problem we	uneasy relationship
always create a new problem to solve	man and machine
	assembly line
We won WWI but it just led to WWII	one more machine part
and Nazism and others	war was stalemated
	hollow victory
	brutal, carnage
	pure misery
	great heroism
	transformed into a cockroach

SET-UP V: QUESTIONS

Another thematic approach to note-taking is to have the students listen to the whole lecture or passage and then compose questions. The questions should not be detailed in nature. Rather, they should address the piece in totality. A good question would be one which you couldn't answer without having heard the whole piece.

TEACHER'S INSTRUCTIONS

Listen to the whole passage without taking any notes. Then, write one or two questions that take in the whole piece. Don't ask questions that require one or two details, or that can be answered in a single sentence. You don't have to answer the questions, but the words you use in your questions should indicate that you've understood the point of the passage.

Questions: late 19th/early 20th centuries

1. *Explain some of the advantages and disadvantages of the scientific and technological developments of this time period.*
2. *How did science and technology affect World War I, and how did World War I lead to important developments in the 1920s?*

FOLLOW-UP

The first order of business to follow-up on is spelling. If we neglect to do that, we have no one but ourselves to blame for spelling that will make our hair fall out in clumps. It takes only a few minutes of class time to provide a topic-related spelling list, especially of names. In so doing, we review the details, killing the proverbial two stones with one bird.

The notes themselves don't necessarily have to be corrected, so as not to create an unreadable mess. A list of correctly spelled words will suffice.

Next, it's a good idea to allow time for the students to amalgamate their notes. That's what the extra space was for.

Finally, because note-taking is a "learning to learn" activity, students should reflect on the effectiveness of particular note-taking styles. The following brief questionnaire can help students to better understand how particular types of note-taking work for them.

NOTE-TAKING STYLES: WHAT WORKS?

Topic:_____

Note-taking style:_____

Did you take complete notes?_____

Were you able to keep up with the pace of the notes and lecture?_____

Did you refer to your notes after class for any of the following purposes?

- ♦ Review for quiz: _____
- ♦ Review for test: _____
- ♦ Essay: _____

Would you use this style of note-taking again? _____

What classes or topics is this style of note-taking most useful for? _____

_____

SUMMARY

Note-taking is an essential skill for academic life and for the workplace. Effective note-taking depends on paperwork management. Teachers across the board should oversee note-taking, giving feedback regarding organization, legibility, and completeness.

Notes are useful to the extent that they keep learners on task during class and serve as a review for future reference. Learners need to have a personal interest in their notes, believing that taking notes is not just a teacher-imposed exercise, but a way to involve themselves in their learning.

There's more to taking notes than verbatim copying. Nor is it enough to simply deliver a lecture and instruct students to "take notes." This chapter has presented five models that show how different forms of note-taking can direct various approaches to a text.

10

WRITING CENTERS

CHAPTER OVERVIEW

Writing centers provide services to students who need remediation or want advancement in their writing skills. In this chapter, I describe several paradigms for such centers:

- ◆ Tutorial instruction
- ◆ Curriculum-based instruction
- ◆ Project-based instruction
- ◆ Prescriptive-based instruction
- ◆ Push-in instruction
- ◆ Combinations

To evaluate your writing center and consider how it might be restructured, start by considering the following:

- ◆ **Personnel**

  Who teaches in the writing center? An English teacher? A special education teacher? A content area teacher? Is the center staffed by the same person(s) all day, or are department members assigned to staff the center during part of their regular schedule? Are paraprofessionals part of the staff, and if so, do they interact with the students?

- ◆ **Communication**

  Are there definite times set aside for regular communication between the writing center staff and the regular teachers? Are content area teachers included in such communications, or only English teachers? Or, is communication between the writing center teacher(s) and the regular teachers limited to notes left in mailboxes and quick exchanges at the copy machine and over the lunch table between spoonfuls of fat-free yogurt? Is communication bogged down or enhanced by institutionalized paperwork? What happens when regular classroom teachers and writing center staff disagree about issues related to writing or pedagogy? How are conflicts resolved?

♦ **Students**

How do students find their way to the writing center? Are they mandated to receive remedial services so that they can pass the state tests? Do they sign themselves in? Is it a stable group? Walk-ins? Sign-ups? Is the group heterogeneous? Do students interact with each other? If so, how is their interaction mediated by the staff? Are there expectations? Homework? Do they receive a grade for their participation? Do they keep records of their progress? How much autonomy do students have in the writing center? Has it degenerated to a glorified study hall? Is there, as they say inside the beltway, an exit strategy?

♦ **Environment and Resources**

Is the writing center an inviting place to enter? Does its furniture allow for recombinations of groups of students as well as individual work? Are there any semiprivate areas? Are there headphones? Ample computer stations? Is it located near the library-media center? Plenty of handbooks, dictionaries, and other reference materials for students who are not working on computers? Are the walls filled with cues for writing?

♦ **Administration and Evaluation of Program?**

Is there a written mission statement for the writing center? If so, does the reality match the vision? Who has authority to make changes? Whose input goes into the changes? Is the writing center an arm of the English department, or does it service content area writing as well? To what extent are building administrators and department chairs involved in the workings of the center? Does the center receive an adequate budget through a separate line, or does it take alms from the departments? Do the staff feel secure in their positions or are they anxious about their expendability? If so, does this insecurity result in ever-changing personnel? Is data collected in a professional manner so as to justify the success of the center?

As you read these questions, you may realize that your writing center could be servicing students in better ways. It may be time to adjust your paradigm. Here are five forms of writing centers, along with pros and cons.

TUTORIALS

Many writing centers function as places where students can go for "extra help" with their writing. This usually amounts to a homework center. Maybe students are scheduled on the days when they don't have physical education classes or labs. Maybe they sign themselves in out of study hall or are referred by teachers in their regular classes, usually English and social studies. Maybe the writing center is called a learning center and offers assistance in all subjects.

Maybe the center works primarily to effect success in state tests and services students who failed, or came close to failing, benchmark tests.

The advantages of the tutorial paradigm are flexibility, individual attention, and immediate relationship between need and service. From an administrative viewpoint, the teachers who staff the tutorial center are seen as having a lighter load than regular classroom teachers. In some contracts, writing center teachers are allowed to work one more period than classroom teachers. Service in the writing center may not count as a preparation. If a positive relationship exists between the writing center teacher and the student, the tutorial model is good for public relations. Even better public relations develop when the writing center teacher communicates with, and may run interference for, parents. And the students' grades could go up as a direct result of the tutorials, which is, of course, the most measurable sign of success.

On the other hand, the tutorial model may not be making the most of what a writing center can do. It can become little other than a homework center. The writing center teacher can feel discouraged and unenergized because he feels that he is carrying out the work of other teachers all day. He may feel conflicted because students bring him poorly designed writing tasks in which his colleagues have not displayed a high level of scholarship in the directions themselves. Administrators may find themselves in the middle of disputes between colleagues and departments. When you work with students one-on-one, it's easy to see things from their perspective, perhaps too much. Some writing center teachers come to see their role as advocating for the student at the expense of collegial harmony, only to find that the student was at fault in the first place. After working in a tutorial atmosphere for a year, many writing center teachers itch for the dynamics of the regular classroom, where they feel more professional autonomy and satisfaction.

Tutorial centers require a lot of resources because students will be on their own much of the time. In the absence of such resources, students become distracted (which they may do in the presence of such resources as well). The teacher comes to feel like a floor supervisor, constantly disciplining students for being off-task.

Sometimes, writing center teachers try to intervene with mini-lessons at the beginning of class. This practice does set the tone and focus for academic work. However, students don't always welcome whole-class instruction, even for just a few minutes, which they see as taking away from *their time* to complete their homework. If the student is coming to the writing center voluntarily, he may just return to study hall where no one bothers (teaches) him.

CURRICULUM-BASED INSTRUCTION

Not all writing centers are unstructured tutorial centers. Some operate by delivering a lesson series to a cohort of students. That cohort rotates through the writing center, either on a twice-a-week basis throughout the year or in cycles that can last for any number of weeks.

Teachers who run curriculum-based writing centers believe that students need definite instruction on the component skills of writing. They might group students according to performance on standardized tests that involve writing or according to classroom performance.

It makes sense to build instruction around the school's common rubric. Suppose you have a curriculum-based writing center that meets with a cohort of students 50 times (every day for 10 weeks). Here is what their lesson schedule might look like.

LESSONS 1-10: ADDRESSING THE TASK

The students learn how to focus first and foremost on what the question of the task is requiring them to do. They analyze the components of the question. They come to understand the implications of key task verbs such as *explain, discuss, compare, evaluate,* and so on. They build word banks for each of the key task verbs.

For teachers to be successful in the writing center, they need to communicate with the subject area teachers who are assigning and assessing writing tasks. Some common task verbs are ambiguous. If by the word *discuss* one teacher expects an examination of both sides of a controversy but another teacher expects the defense of one point of view on a controversy, then students may innocently deliver the wrong kind of response. *Discuss* is not the best task verb because it is so broad. Do you want the student to illuminate the issue? Explain various sides of it? Give the background? Avoid the word *discuss* as your task verb unless you clarify what kind of discussion you expect.

Another troublesome task verb is *compare*. Do you want similarities or differences? Do *compare* and *contrast* really mean different things, or do you want the student to find similarities between unlike things and dissimilarities between like things? Comparison-contrast writing can be done point-by-point or block style. The former brings both subjects together in each paragraph, comparing them on a particular point. The latter discusses one topic thoroughly, then moves to the other, then makes points of comparison, or simply expects the reader to draw conclusions about what is similar and what is different.

Lessons in *addressing the task*, then, train students in the mature habit of mind of really analyzing reader expectation, audience, and purpose before they begin to write.

LESSONS 11-20: DEVELOPMENT

The students learn how to provide a focused main idea and sufficient detail to thoroughly answer the question. They learn about various kinds of development in content area writing: reasons, examples, data, quotations, evidence, textual reference, facts, and hypotheses.

The paragraph is the basic unit of complete thought in informational writing. Teachers may begin by giving students all but one sentence in a well-developed paragraph. The students then have to supply a sentence that will complete the paragraph. From there, students learn to develop paragraphs from a topic sentence alone.

LESSONS 21-30: ORGANIZATION

As you can see, the lessons in this series are flow naturally from one to the next. Now that the student is focused on the task, now that she understands what development of paragraphs is all about, she is ready to assist the reader by presenting ideas in an organized format, including transitions.

These lessons give the students practice in using various kinds of graphic organizers and traditional outlines. Other subskills are effective repetition, use of textual features to help the reader, and organizational cuing words that guide the reader gently from one idea to the next.

LESSONS 31-40: LANGUAGE

For the past six weeks, the student has been using language, of course. But she may be using informal language. Academic teachers want academic words and formal language. The lessons in this segment strengthen the students' vocabulary by teaching Latin-based prefixes, roots, and suffixes. And these lessons also reinforce the importance of ridding academic language of slang, colloquialisms, and short-cuts that are unwelcome in academic writing.

LESSONS 41-50: GSPC (GRAMMAR, SPELLING, PUNCTUATION, CAPITALIZATION)

These lessons go over the main grammatical offenses, major spelling rules, punctuation guidelines, and capitalization conventions. The writing center teacher does not address rules, guidelines and errors in two weeks as the English teacher in a regular class might do. In two weeks, the writing center teacher can cover only the most noticeable and common transgressions:

♦ Complete sentences
♦ Possessive apostrophes
♦ Basic comma rules
♦ *IE* and *EI*
♦ Adding prefixes and suffixes
♦ Words with sc
♦ Basic capitalization rules
♦ Spelling of academic words that have Greek letter combinations: *ch, ph, psy, kn*
♦ Sentence clarity through elimination of wordiness
♦ Textual clarity through unambiguous pronoun reference

Some curriculum-based writing centers organize their lessons around genres:

- Writing the document-based question essay
- Writing lab reports
- Writing constructed responses to test questions (one or two sentences)
- Answering end-of-chapter questions from the textbook

Still others organize lessons around study skills:

- Writing the Harvard outline
- Note-taking
- Dialectical journaling
- Study cards

PROJECT-BASED WRITING CENTERS

Using the same structure in which a cohort of students rotates into a writing center for a period of time, some schools have a writing center that takes students through a single project: the research paper. This kind of writing instruction can be carried out by the library-media specialist.

The structure of the project-based writing center has three components:

- Whole-class instruction in which the teacher (librarian) explains the nature of research papers and the procedures for writing them. This instruction includes a detailed tour of the school and public libraries. It also includes a guided tour of Internet resources that facilitate academic research.
- Independent research and writing by the students
- Writing process activities, including guided peer readings with feedback to the writer

These three structures, integrated into the process of writing a research paper, might look like this:

- Selecting and narrowing the topic
- Writing a tentative thesis statement
- Beginning the research
- Refining the thesis statement
- Making an outline
- Continuing research, keeping track of sources used, and making electronic note cards
- Fleshing out paragraphs and transitions

- Writing an abstract
- Writing the works cited page and using parenthetical citations
- Understanding how to avoid plagiarism
- Proofreading
- Production and presentation

The advantage of this kind of writing center is that it sets all students in the school at the same starting point for an important academic genre. This common experience obviates one of our most frustrating problems in teaching writing in the content areas: inconsistent institutional expectations.

PRESCRIPTIVE-BASED INSTRUCTION

A writing center that relies on prescriptive-based instruction is directing students to lessons that will meet demonstrated needs. Although prescriptive-based instruction can be done in a low-tech way, directing students to lessons that are on paper and stored in folders, the best way to operate is through a customized Website.

Such a Website offers a well-organized compilation of activities that students can do to improve their skills. The activities can be self-correcting. The activities can be original ones composed by the teachers as well as links to existing sites.

PUSH-IN INSTRUCTION

At Hendrick Hudson High School in Montrose, New York, where I teach English, we have a model where I have a reduced class load and a floating period in which I visit content area classes to deliver instruction in writing for that class.

I don't have a set curriculum. I meet with interested teachers individually or by department to find out what the immediate needs are and how I can address them in a lesson or two. I then assist the teachers in evaluating the writing when it comes in.

The advantages of this model are many: The content area teacher receives assistance and training in integrating writing-to-learn and writing-for-assessment. I, as an English teacher, develop an understanding of the kinds of writing (and reading) that my students do in other parts of their academic lives, and I bring that insight into my own classroom instruction. These advantages are purely functional, but a bonus is that sometimes I can interest my colleagues in the science department to bring in some literary science writing. Essayists like Annie Dillard, Lewis Thomas, Verlyn Klinkengborg and novelists like James Michener are "poets of science." For many students, the path to motivation in science is the beauty of its language.

COMBINATIONS

These writing center paradigms are by no means mutually exclusive. The purpose and structure of the writing center can change on a semester or quarterly basis. Its mornings can be different from its afternoons. It can be one model on Mondays, Wednesdays, and Fridays; another on Tuesdays and Thursdays. It can be staffed by an English teacher who is well-versed in content area writing genres, a content area teacher who is well-versed in writing pedagogy, or a special education teacher. Other learning specialists, most notably the librarian, can make guest appearances.

CONCLUSION

The keys to successful writing centers that promote writing in the content areas are an interdisciplinary attitude toward writing, communication, administrative support, and student accountability. It's important to think of the writing center as an evolving model, responding to governmental requirements, changing demographics in a district, and new technology. If your writing center is the same now as it was five years ago, you might want to give it a makeover, or at least a new paint job.

A WORKSHOP FOR TEACHERS

WRITING IN THE CONTENT AREAS: WHY? WHAT? HOW?

WHY?

We integrate writing in the content areas because writing makes people smarter.

Our students won't remember most of the *facts* that we teach them, just as we don't remember the details of what we learned as students. But learning that lasts is learning to engage in the habits of mind that *make us smart*. Writing does that. Writing makes people smart because writers connect the dots in their learning. They put their thoughts on paper. They have a sustained conversation with themselves, and from that conversation they discover what they think. Writing helps us understand what we know.

Writing opens and trains the mind. By writing, we use new terminology and process new learning by linking new knowledge to prior knowledge. Writing accesses memory and imprints memory. It allows students to make personal meaning out of information. And writing allows teachers to understand how students are thinking.

Writing breeds academic success. Writers become better readers; readers become better writers. Writing stiffens the backbone of a class: Students respect a class that requires serious writing. Classes that include a writing component become varied, interesting, rigorous, empowering, meaningful, memorable, and important.

WHAT AND HOW?

We can divide academic writing into two camps: writing to learn and writing for assessment. The former is writing to find out what you are learning, to have what you are learning make sense to you; the latter is showing what you have learned. These two camps are overlapping and interdependent.

We can think of writing to learn as having five modes:

+ Writing to make connections
+ Writing to understand and clarify
+ Writing to crystallize and remember
+ Writing to make an argument
+ Writing to try out new language

WRITING TO MAKE CONNECTIONS

When we make Venn diagrams to illustrate similarities and differences, we are using an informal writing genre to help us understand. We make connections in an informal writing mode when we make timelines, write journals, label diagrams, make mind maps or cluster diagrams, and use other kinds of graphic organizers.

Content area teachers may think their students are "not writing a lot" when in fact they are using all kinds of effective meaning-making writing activities that are informal. These informal writing activities are invaluable to students as they process new knowledge.

How?

Some writing-to-learn activities promote making connections:

+ Venn diagrams
+ Finding similarities between disparate things
+ Finding dissimilarities between similar things
+ Explaining cause and effect
+ Linking events in a sequence
+ Journalizing: Making text-to-self connections
+ Journalizing: Making text-to-world connections

WRITING TO UNDERSTAND AND CLARIFY

Students write to understand and clarify in various tried-and-true ways that are staples in most classrooms: the traditional Harvard outline, paraphrases, summaries, chapter questions, and definitions of key terms.

Some writing tasks require a type of role playing. This means that the student takes on the first person voice of a historical figure (major or minor) and explains how historical events affect him or her in everyday life or over time. First-person writing can be helpful for students in science and math, as they explain how to solve a problem, or put themselves right inside the problem or process and explain their way out of it.

All writing, by its nature of putting knowledge into words and getting those words onto paper one word at a time, illuminates thinking. Often, we don't know what we think until we write it. Similarly, we may think we understand something that we "just can't put into words" only to discover that if we can't write something, we don't truly know it. We call this phenomenon, where writing is the handmaiden of thought, "writing ourselves into knowing."

How?

Some writing-to-learn activities promote understanding and clarification:
- Traditional Harvard outline
- Summaries
- Paraphrasing
- Identification of key terms
- Identifying the questions that the text answers

WRITING TO ORGANIZE AND REMEMBER

The act of writing is itself an organizational and memory aid. Students write not only to organize and remember the content itself, but also to organize and remember their own learning needs. We make "to do" lists to ease our minds. Once an item is committed on paper to the "to do" list, we can relax about it, having prioritized it and knowing that it will get done.

To organize, we need main ideas and subordinating ideas. This is the way that paragraphs are structured. To organize, we need to separate like things from unlike things, in accordance with an organizing principle. Imagine a deck of playing cards laid face up on a table. Your organizing principle could be suits, or it could be pictures and non-pictures, or it could be even numbers and odd numbers. You could organize the fifty-two items in any number of ways, and your system would be valid *so long as you declared your organizing principle*. Think of all the ways in which students could understand your subject if they thought in terms of organizing principles and could explain them in writing. And think about how much the process of setting forth organizing principles would help them remember the information.

How?

Some writing-to-learn activities facilitate organization and memory:
- Venn diagram
- T chart
- Tree and branch
- Cluster diagram
- Fishbone (main idea as the spine and subordinating ideas as the bones)

WRITING TO MAKE AN ARGUMENT

One organizing principle of language is by rhetorical purpose: *to inform, to persuade,* or *to entertain.* Much of content area writing, and writing in English class as well, is persuasive writing, the setting forth of an argument. Aristotle posited that argument rests upon a tripod of *ethos, logos,* and *pathos.* Ethos arises from the credibility of the person making the argument: how is this person using language in a way that causes the reader to have faith or doubt in his or her worthiness to make this argument? Logos arises from the logic of the argument, its syllogisms, causal relationships, and supportive evidence. And pathos arises from the purely emotional impact that the argument evokes.

Effective argument must be organized. We usually teach novices to write a thesis statement, and that thesis statement is most effectively stated as a sentence whose verb is a form of *to be.* Logicians call such a statement a categorical proposition. Once the categorical proposition is nailed down, the writer does his or her best to prove it, all the while maintaining credibility and amicability with the intended audience.

How?

Some writing-to-learn activities that promote argumentation skills:

- Classic argumentation essay
- Classic debate format
- Audience-directed writings
- Thesis statement and support
- Categorical propositions

WRITING TO TRY OUT NEW LANGUAGE

When we learn a subject, we are learning to speak a new language. It isn't enough to listen to the teacher use subject language, nor is it enough to read it in the textbook. Nor is it enough to manipulate the new language on a multiple choice or fill-in-the-blank test. Language has to be used, formed into sentences.

When we ask students to look up words on a list in the glossary and then use the words in a sentence, that isn't giving them enough context. The sentence needs substance, action, and visuals. Ask students to use new words in sentences that have at least fifteen words, at least one action verb, and a visual image for the reader.

Highlight new words and new phrases. Make an educated guess about their meanings. Then, confirm your guess.

How?

Some writing-to-learn activities access new language:

♦ Write an original sentence with your new language. The sentence should:
  • Tell a story (beginning, middle, end)
  • Include a visual.
  • Have a person as its subject
  • Have an action verb

♦ Break words down by prefix, root, suffix

WRITING FOR ASSESSMENT: FRAMING THE TASK, SCORING THE TASK

If you are assigning writing on a test or as homework, think of assessment at the same time that you frame the task. What learning outcomes are you looking for? Include these on your scoring guide (rubric). Give out the scoring guide at the same time that you give the assignment. Students should use it just as the name says: as a guide.

Your task should be framed so that the student has some latitude, preferably some choice. We feel more invested when we've had a choice, but too much choice inhibits us. Avoid the kinds of tasks that can be cut and pasted. Use a service such as Turnitin.com to test for plagiarism, and tell the students that you are doing so.

Finally, think about follow-up. How is the student who gives you a deficient piece going to meet your standards? Having even a simple Website with a minimal number of prescriptive lessons to which you can refer students is valuable.

PRACTICE AND PERSISTENCE

Make writing a fixture in your classroom. Include a variety of experiences, formal and informal, structured and unstructured, graded and not graded, to allow students to process, reinforce, apply, and remember what you've taught them.